LINDSAY KEMENY

7 MIGHTY MOVES

*Research-Backed, Classroom-Tested Strategies
to Ensure K-to-3 Reading Success*

■SCHOLASTIC

For Nathan

All of this is possible because of you. Thank you for igniting the spark.
Keep using your brave voice!

Senior Vice President and Publisher: Tara Welty
Editorial Director: Sarah Longhi
Development Editor: Raymond Coutu
Senior Editor: Shelley Griffin
Production Editor: Danny Miller
Creative Director: Tannaz Fassihi
Interior Designer: Maria Lilja

Scholastic is not responsible for the content of third-party websites and does not endorse any site or imply that the information on the site is error-free, correct, accurate, or reliable.

Cover illustration by Giulia Neri.

Photos: 80 (left): © Alexandr Ermolaev/Dreamstime; 80 (right), 121, 123, 142, 150: © Shutterstock.com. Icons created by The Noun Project. All other photos courtesy of Lindsay and Steven Kemeny.

Credits: 9: "The Reading Rope" by H. S. Scarborough from "Connecting Early Language and Literacy to Later Reading (Dis) Abilities: Evidence, Theory, and Practice," originally published in *Handbook of Early Literacy Research, Volume 1*. Copyright © 2001 by Guilford Press. Reprinted by permission; 16, 19: "English Consonant Phonemes by Place and Manner of Articulation" and "English Vowel Phonemes by Order of Articulation" from *Speech to Print: Language Essentials for Teachers, Third Edition* by Louisa Cook Moats, Ed.D. Copyright © 2020 by Paul H. Brookes Publishing Co., Inc. Reprinted by permission; 27: lyrics from "Break It Down" © Erica Allen-Jameson. Reprinted by permission of the author; 46: *UFLI Foundations* "Scope & Sequence" by Holly B. Lane © University of Florida Literacy Institute. Reprinted courtesy of Dr. Holly Lane; 46: *Scholastic Ready4Reading*® "Scope & Sequence" copyright © 2023 by Scholastic Inc. Reprinted by permission; 72: "Decoding Dragon" copyright © 2019 by Lyn Stone. Reprinted by permission of the author; 80, 82–84, 124: pages from "Decodable Texts" © Scholastic Inc. Reprinted with permission; 100: "First Dolch Word List" by Katharine Pace Miles, Gregory B. Rubin, and Selenid Gonzalez-Frey from "Rethinking Sight Words" published in *The Reading Teacher*, Volume 71. Copyright © 2017 by International Literacy Association. Reprinted by permission of John Wiley & Sons, Inc.; 112: "Oral Reading Fluency Norms" by Jan Hasbrouck and Gerald Tindal from "An Update to Compiled ORF Norms" (Technical Report #1702). Copyright © 2017 by Behavioral Research and Teaching, University of Oregon. Reprinted courtesy of Dr. Gerald Tindal; 135: "Sample Oral Language Unit" from "The Importance of Oral Language in Literacy and the Impact on Third-Grade Student Writing" copyright © 2022 by Mary Allison Peck. Reprinted courtesy of Dr. Allison Peck; 145–146: "Sophisticated Words" sample charts by Holly B. Lane and Stephanie Arriaza Allen from "The Vocabulary-Rich Classroom: Modeling Sophisticated Word Use to Promote Word Consciousness and Vocabulary Growth" published in *The Reading Teacher*, Volume 63. Copyright © 2010 by International Literacy Association. Reprinted by permission of John Wiley & Sons, Inc.
All rights reserved.

4 5 6 7 8 9 10   40   32 31 30 29 28 27 26 25 24 23

Scholastic Inc., 557 Broadway, New York, NY 10012

Contents

Acknowledgments

I am grateful to my family members for their support and encouragement, and for giving me the space to write, rewrite, and revise. Steve, thank you for being with me every step of the way, offering advice and motivation, and taking care of the family so I could focus on writing. Austin, thank you for being a sounding board, patiently listening as I expressed my ideas, experiences, and feelings. Jack, I appreciate your sincere interest in the work, and how you continually asked for updates and if that "book thing" was still happening. Nathan, I loved writing with you curled up next to me on the couch. Thank you for your enthusiasm and eagerness to share my book with your teachers. Aubrey, thank you for your unwavering love and affection. I'm happy that I've inspired you to write your own books, and I enjoyed occasions when we were writing at the same time.

I am so thankful to my students, past and present, for everything they have taught me. It brings me so much joy to teach them every single day.

My heartfelt appreciation goes to Anita Archer! It is such an honor to have someone I admire so greatly write the foreword to my book, and I so appreciate her time and kind words.

I have incredible respect and gratitude for Pam Kastner, who not only reviewed one of my draft chapters, but went on to review the entire manuscript. Pam, your support means the world to me, and your kind words have brought tears to my eyes more than once.

I will be forever grateful to all those who reviewed a draft chapter or two! Thank you so much for your attention to detail, encouragement, and expert advice: Matt Burns, Anna Geiger, Margaret Goldberg, Lorraine Griffith, Nancy Hennessy, Stacy Hurst, Janice Kohler-Curtis, Meredith Nardone, and Stephanie Stollar. Lorraine, thank you for the brilliant "Keep, Stop, Start" idea and your support from the very beginning of this project.

I am lucky to have had such an amazing editor, Ray Coutu, who offered great advice, asked the hard questions, and helped turn my writing into the best that it could be. Thank you, Ray! And thank you to the entire Scholastic team, including Sarah Longhi and Tara Welty, along with many others. Thank you for all your work on this book and for believing in me and my vision.

There are so many amazing educators who have helped shape me into the teacher I am today. Thank you! I am also grateful to my principal, Meggan Nichols, who has supported my growth in the science of reading and who continues to support me as I implement these "mighty moves" in my classroom.

Thank you to the many others who I've consulted for opinions and suggestions, including Julia Lindsey, Nick Wells, Kate Winn, and my parents, siblings, extended family members, and friends. Thank you for your input and all the title brainstorm sessions! Troy, I got your name in the book after all! And Kev, sorry your title suggestion, *Read*, didn't make the cut!

Foreword
by Anita L. Archer

The science of reading is the body of scientifically based research conducted over the last five decades that informs us on how reading should be taught. Its Big Ideas have been settled throughout my career: during my years teaching elementary school, training teachers at universities, speaking across the country, developing interventions for struggling readers, and consulting with districts. Yes, the Big Ideas were known. However, they were not implemented universally and are still not, though there are signs we are getting better.

Often, we've gone down the wrong path,

- hoping that focusing on the love of reading would lead to skilled readers when the opposite is true: the mastery of reading skills leads to lovers of reading.
- believing that readers decode unfamiliar words by guessing based on available pictures and context, when the truth is that proficient readers look at the letters in words and rely on letter/sound associations to determine pronunciations.
- thinking that students would discover letter/sound associations when very systematic, intentional teaching of phonics benefits the decoding and encoding of students.

We knew better but we didn't always do better.

Today, spurred by the reality that one out of three third graders is reading below grade level, we realize that effective reading instruction in the primary grades establishes the foundation of reading competency, and we are inspired by professional training in the science of reading that is flowing across our country, states, districts, and schools, as well as the parents who are shouting, "We can do better! We must do better!" Our children deserve to read accurately and fluently with excellent comprehension as they ascend in the grades. We will do better!

And that brings me to this book and its author. Lindsay Kemeny is a devoted mother of a son with dyslexia, exemplary primary teacher, dedicated research sleuth, passionate advocate for children, and wise coach. Her son's and students' struggles with learning to read were the impetus for her search for better, research-backed practices. As her knowledge increased and her students' reading levels soared, she began to share good practices by blogging, podcasting, and finally writing this book. But the voice you will hear as you read *7 Mighty Moves* is that of a passionate, wise coach who speaks directly to you, the teacher who transforms students into READERS.

As I finished the book, I envisioned a virtual school walk-through with you. For a moment, pretend you are on a leadership team. The primary teachers have read *7 Mighty Moves*, discussed each chapter in a PLC, analyzed their current instruction, and implemented Lindsay's recommended moves.

First Stop: The kindergarten teacher is beginning her whole-class phonics lesson with a short phonemic awareness activity on blending sounds into words. She has established instructional routines, elicits choral responses, and monitors student performance and gives feedback to the class. In the debrief, she explains that phonemic awareness is also embedded in decoding and encoding activities.

Second Stop: We are now entering a first-grade class to observe the teacher's whole-class phonics lesson from a research-based program recently adopted by the district. First, the teacher briskly reviews previously taught letter/sound associations and CVC words. Next, he introduces the sound that the letter *o* represents, a new phoneme/grapheme relationship. Then, he models how to sound out a word using continuous blending and guides students in sounding out words. The emerging readers are engaged and accurate.

Third Stop: The third stop is a second grade. The teacher is working with a small group of students who are rereading a decodable passage. She prepares students by reviewing the irregular words *again* and *women*, pointing out the "tricky part" in each one and reminding students to keep their eyes on the words, no guessing. Next, students whisper-read the passage as the teacher monitors each one and provides feedback. Finally, students partner-read as the teacher continues to monitor and provide feedback. So much reading in a short amount of time.

Fourth Stop: Before lunch, one more stop: third grade. The students are gathered on the rug, the teacher is perched on a stool, and the nearby wall is covered with all-things oceans: covers of books about oceans, a world map with oceans highlighted, ocean word lists, and an ocean facts poster. To launch the new book, the teacher reads its title and analyzes its cover with the students. Next, he introduces the term, *nautical*. As the teacher reads the book, he stops and asks questions. After the reading, students tell their partners five ocean facts they recall.

Walk-throughs at your school will be this rich if you and your colleagues implement Lindsay's *7 Mighty Moves*, and your students will learn and read as they never have before.

Read on. Teach on. Celebrate.

Introduction

I f it hadn't been for my son's struggles, I don't think I would have ever fully learned the things I know about teaching reading. I had known from the time he was very young that learning was difficult for him but was unsure what to do. I read to him daily from the time he was a baby and had tried all the techniques I was taught in college and my early years of teaching. Nothing seemed to help. When he entered kindergarten, I felt a sense of desperation when I realized that I, a teacher, had no idea how to help him. Eventually, he was diagnosed with severe dyslexia and depression. I didn't realize the depths of his pain until months later when he began sobbing regularly about his reading struggles. I held him in my arms, trying to comfort him as he shared harrowing thoughts. I soon discovered that my son was not alone; many people who struggle to read, young and old, grapple with the same feelings of inadequacy. The ability to read is so tightly connected to how we feel about ourselves. Literacy leader Tracy Weeden said, "When we read, we can think critically, we can make decisions, we can shape change" (2022). How inspiring that we teachers can have such an impact on our students' lives. When we teach our students to read, we open windows of opportunity for them. But that can only happen if we consider the needs of all students, keep our expectations high, and provide them with the skills to become literate members of society.

My son's diagnosis sparked a flame inside me to find out all I could about dyslexia and effective reading instruction for all students— those with dyslexia and those without it. I needed to help him, and I needed to prevent other children from experiencing the shame and embarrassment that he did. So, I learned all I could about the science behind reading and began to rethink the strategies and methods that I had been taught. The more I learned, the more questions I had. Why wasn't I taught that science in college? Why was I never told about the National Reading Panel (2000)? Why didn't any of my professors show me how to find and read research studies? I felt betrayed and misled. Why was the science of reading being largely ignored?

> When we teach our students to read, we open windows of opportunity for them. But that can only happen if we consider the needs of all students, keep our expectations high, and provide them with the skills to become literate members of society.

What Is the Science of Reading?

Sometimes, educators think the science of reading refers to a specific curriculum, program, or method. But the term actually refers to a large body of high-quality research on reading. It encompasses thousands of studies. Or, as literacy expert Louisa Moats puts it, "'The science of reading' is not an ideology, a philosophy, a political agenda, a one-size-fits-all approach, a program of instruction, or a specific component of instruction. It is the emerging consensus from many related disciplines, based on literally thousands of studies, supported by hundreds of millions of research dollars, conducted across the world in many languages" (2019). The Reading League has an excellent resource for understanding the science of reading entitled, "Science of Reading: Defining Guide." This free download is available on their website (thereadingleague.org).

My Journey to Effective Reading Instruction

I was taught that reading develops naturally and that my students would grow into readers if I surrounded them with great books and encouraged a love of reading. But as I dug deeper into research, I started to rethink that idea. Did I stop surrounding my students with great books and encouraging a love of reading? No! But, unlike oral language, I learned that written language is a code and students need to crack that code to become readers. They need to understand how the words they say and sounds they hear connect with the words and letters on the page. Many students need direct and explicit instruction in that code to develop as readers. One of my favorite quotes is from cognitive psychologist Steven Pinker. He says, "Children are wired for sound, but print is an optional accessory that must be painstakingly bolted on" (as cited in Wolf, 2008). Some students will need much stronger bolts than others, especially those with learning differences such as dyslexia. And while some of our students will learn to read regardless of the approach we use, many more of them will likely *only* become proficient if we use the methods aligned with science (Torgesen, 2000; Scanlon et al., 2005). We cannot turn our backs on those students. We cannot limit their potential.

As I continued my journey, I learned that cracking the code is not all students need to become readers! Psychologist and literacy expert Hollis Scarborough (2001) taught me the many components students need to become proficient readers. On a daily basis, I think about how I can address all the strands in her Reading Rope in my instruction. More on the Reading Rope in Move 7, page 129.

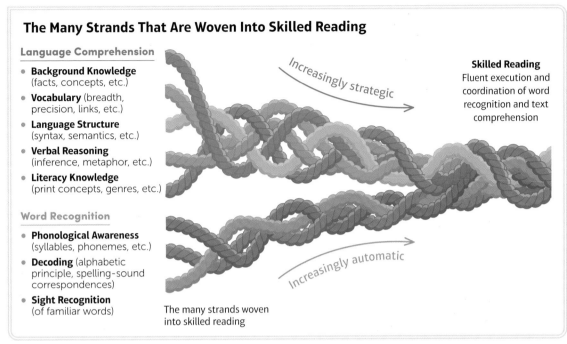

The Many Strands That Are Woven Into Skilled Reading

Language Comprehension

- **Background Knowledge** (facts, concepts, etc.)
- **Vocabulary** (breadth, precision, links, etc.)
- **Language Structure** (syntax, semantics, etc.)
- **Verbal Reasoning** (inference, metaphor, etc.)
- **Literacy Knowledge** (print concepts, genres, etc.)

Word Recognition

- **Phonological Awareness** (syllables, phonemes, etc.)
- **Decoding** (alphabetic principle, spelling-sound correspondences)
- **Sight Recognition** (of familiar words)

Increasingly strategic

Skilled Reading Fluent execution and coordination of word recognition and text comprehension

Increasingly automatic

The many strands woven into skilled reading

The Reading Rope (Scarborough, 2001)

Changing Course at Home

Once I had a stronger grasp of effective reading instruction, I began to tutor my son. With time, patience, and effort on both our parts, he began making steady progress. As his reading improved, so did his self-esteem. He is not only coming to terms with his learning differences, but also embracing them. The fractures in his heart are healing and his confidence is growing. While I have done a lot to ease my son's depression, the ability to read has helped him the most.

Changing Course at School

With my stronger grasp on reading instruction, I also began to apply the things I was learning in my kindergarten classroom. The difference was striking. I saw firsthand the effects science-based practice can have. Each change I made impacted my students in a positive way. And, in the process, I gained clarity and confidence. I no longer wondered why some students struggled to read, while others didn't. I learned how to take a close look at my students, determine their exact strengths and weaknesses, and adjust my instruction accordingly. It was exciting to realize that, as a kindergarten teacher, I could prevent many reading difficulties by providing research-based instruction that would set up my students for success.

My journey continued when I moved to second grade. At that point, I wasn't just preventing reading difficulties, but remediating them. I learned just how important it is to intervene right away rather than waiting for students to improve on their own. Now I'm teaching first grade and love the immense growth students show at this age.

With each grade I've taught, I have continued to learn, grow, and adjust my practice. I am constantly rethinking and refining. As my teaching improves, so does my students' learning. I assess my students and analyze the results regularly. This helps me understand if my instruction is working for each student and what needs to be adjusted. Each year, the scores get a little better. Last year, my students had phenomenal growth rates, which was essential because over half of them started the year well below benchmark. My knowledge of the science of reading and applying it in the classroom has made all the difference.

Looking to the Horizon

The future of our students who struggle to read does not need to be bleak. We have reason to be hopeful. We can turn the tide. We can teach in a way that will help all our students and, in doing so, prevent illiteracy. I have been asked if, one day, I would like to go into an area of education outside the classroom. At this point, the answer is no. I need to be on the front line, preventing and problem-solving reading difficulties as much as I can.

About This Book

7 Mighty Moves focuses on seven essential areas of primary reading. The moves represent changes I made in those areas after learning about effective reading instruction.

Each move follows a four-part structure:

1. A clear explanation of the move that includes an overview of the research on it and concepts related to it
2. A discussion of "Instructional Implications" to consider as you apply the research in your classrooms
3. "Strategies for Success," my favorite ways to help students acquire necessary reading skills. As such, they truly are "classroom-tested."
4. A summary of key takeaways to remember

As we think about changing our reading instruction, we often think about practices to add. However, we also should think about practices we need to stop

The 7 Mighty Moves		
	From	**To**
Move 1	teaching phonemic awareness randomly	teaching it with intention
Move 2	teaching phonics incidentally and haphazardly	teaching it explicitly and systematically
Move 3	teaching cueing strategies	teaching decoding strategies
Move 4	using predictable texts for beginning readers	using decodable texts for beginning readers
Move 5	encouraging whole-word memorizing of "sight words"	encouraging decoding of high-frequency words
Move 6	expecting fluency to improve on its own	expecting it to improve with meaningful practice opportunities
Move 7	neglecting vocabulary and background knowledge	embracing them to improve comprehension

doing. Sometimes, applying research means abandoning techniques we've come to rely on for years. This is often the hardest part of bringing research to practice: untangling the web of misinformation from our instruction. Each chapter's final section suggests practices to keep doing, stop doing, and start doing. We need to turn our backs on some practices because they may be doing harm to our students. In this book, I describe the practices to abandon and share ones that can have life-changing effects on our students.

It's easy to feel discouraged, defensive, overwhelmed, and even guilty for ineffective methods you've used in the past. I know because I have been there. I have made many mistakes. So, I urge you to take a moment to step back, take a deep breath, and use this book as a springboard into learning more about the science of reading and the research that informs it. Look ahead rather than back. Learn more and move forward. As Maya Angelou said, "Do the best you can until you know better. Then when you know better, do better." Live by her words. Let them comfort you as you recognize that, yes, you were doing the best you could with the knowledge you had. Show compassion for yourself and others. Propel yourself forward for the sake of your current and future students. After all, they count on you to equip them to make a difference in the world.

7 Mighty Moves comes with Lindsay Kemeny's demonstration videos and downloadable teaching resources. You can access them two ways:

1. Scan the QR codes throughout the book.

2. Go to the companion website at scholastic.com/7MMResources.

Teach Phonemic Awareness With Intention

Have you ever heard a child correctly identify the sounds in a word such as *dog*, /d/ /ŏ/ /g/, but then look up at you and say a completely different word, such as *horse*? This demonstrates a weakness in phonemic awareness, a critical component for reading and writing. Students need to be aware of, and consciously think about, the individual speech sounds (phonemes) of our language. They need to be able to blend those sounds together to read the word and pull those sounds apart to spell the word. Experts say the most common source of reading difficulties is poor phonemic awareness (Blachman, 1995; Hulme et al., 2012; Kilpatrick, 2016; Stanovich, 1988; Vellutino et al., 2004).

Becoming aware of that was a turning point for me. It was not something I had learned about in college or my early years of teaching, so intentional instruction in phonemic awareness was a huge shift in my practice. Once I started implementing it, my students' reading and writing skills improved greatly. Studies confirm that as phonemic awareness improves, phonics skills improve as well (Lane & Pullen, 2004). Additionally, explicit instruction in phonemic awareness beginning in kindergarten can actually prevent reading problems. That fact was encouraging to me when I taught kindergarten and even now, as I teach first grade. Whole-class phonemic awareness instruction in kindergarten and first grade is one of the best preventative measures for future reading failure (Moats & Tolman, 2019). By building a strong foundation in phonemic awareness, we set our students up for reading success. Furthermore, although many educators think of phonemic awareness as a "kindergarten skill," older struggling readers very often have weaknesses in this area and will also benefit from instruction.

Intentional instruction in phonemic awareness was a huge shift in my practice. Once I started implementing it, my students' reading and writing skills improved greatly.

Phonemic Awareness Explained

Let's start by defining some terms.

I often hear teachers use the terms *phonics* and *phonemic awareness* interchangeably, but they are not the same. Phonemic awareness is the understanding that spoken language can be broken down into individual speech sounds (phonemes). When you tie those sounds to print (letters), it then becomes phonics, which is the method we use to teach letter-sound combinations. There is often an overlap of our phonics and phonemic awareness instruction. We need to demonstrate explicitly to students how phonemes (sounds) connect to graphemes (letters). More on that later.

Two other commonly confused terms are phonological awareness and phonemic awareness. Phonological awareness is the umbrella term for the knowledge of sounds in spoken language, which includes larger chunks of sound, such as rimes and syllables, and the smallest units of sound, phonemes. It encompasses both phonemic awareness and phonological sensitivity. As mentioned, phonemic awareness is the ability to recognize, identify, and manipulate individual speech sounds (phonemes) in spoken words. It refers only to the smallest units of speech (such as /t/ /k/). We must explicitly teach to the phoneme level because it directly impacts students' reading and writing (Ball & Blachman, 1991; Lane & Pullen, 2004, NRP, 2000).

Phonological sensitivity is the awareness of the larger units of speech in spoken sounds (onsets, rimes, syllables, and whole words). While children often develop phonological sensitivity before phonemic awareness, they do not have to master the larger units before working on individual phonemes.

Terms to Know

Phonemes: Individual speech sounds

Phonemic Awareness: The understanding that spoken language can be broken down into phonemes

Phonological Awareness: The umbrella term for the knowledge of sounds in spoken language, which includes larger chunks of sound, as well as phonemes

Phonological Sensitivity: The awareness of the larger units of speech in spoken sounds

Phonics: The method we use to teach letter-sound combinations.

Phonemic Awareness Skills

Blending and segmenting are the most critical phonemic awareness skills because they are necessary for reading (decoding) and spelling (encoding).

Blending: After being given individual sounds, the student blends them together to make a word.

TEACHER: /s/ /ŭ/ /n/

STUDENT: sun

Segmenting: After being given a word, the student breaks it into its individual sounds.

TEACHER: Tell me all the sounds in the word black.

STUDENT: /b/ /l/ /ă/ /k/.

Substitution is a more difficult phonemic awareness skill because it includes several steps: phoneme isolation, deletion, addition, and blending.

Substitution: The student changes one sound in a word to create a new word.

TEACHER: Say the word *stop*.

STUDENT: Stop.

TEACHER: Now change the sound /t/ to /l/. What's the new word?

STUDENT: "Slop"

The 44 Phonemes of English

Beginning readers need to first become aware of phonemes (again, the individual sounds in spoken words) and then understand that those phonemes are represented by letters or letter patterns. Understanding that phonemes can be represented by letters or letter patterns is known as the alphabetic principle. There are approximately 44 phonemes in the English language. Understanding them yourself can help you as you intentionally draw students' attention to them, and as you analyze students' reading and spelling errors. The 44 phonemes fall into two categories: consonant phonemes and vowel phonemes. Let's begin with consonant phonemes.

"One of the most important jobs for the teacher of beginning reading or the teacher of students with reading problems is to foster awareness of phonemes (speech sounds) in words and to help children acquire the ability to articulate, compare, segment, and blend those phonemes."

—Louisa Moats

Consonant Phonemes

Consonant phonemes differ from vowel phonemes because their sounds are produced with some type of obstruction (teeth, lips, or tongue) to the airflow. We can group the consonant phonemes according to *place of articulation* and *manner of articulation*. The *place of articulation* refers to where the sound is occurring in the mouth. For example, some sounds are produced at the front of the mouth (e.g., /p/ /b/) and some at the very back (e.g., /k/ /h/).

	Place of Articulation						
	lips	teeth on lips	between teeth	behind teeth	roof of mouth	back of throat	glottis
stop sounds unvoiced / voiced	/p/ /b/			/t/ /d/		/k/ /g/	
nasal sounds	/m/			/n/		/ng/	
fricatives unvoiced / voiced		/f/ /v/	/th/ /<u>th</u>/	/s/ /z/	/sh/ /zh/		/h/
affricates unvoiced / voiced					/ch/ /j/		
glides unvoiced / voiced	/wh/ /w/				/y/		
liquids				/l/	/r/		

Manner of Articulation (left-side vertical label)

English Consonant Phonemes by Place and Manner of Articulation (Moats, 2020)

The *manner of articulation* refers to what is happening with our lips, teeth, tongue, and airflow as we produce the sound. Let's take a closer look at each of these subcategories.

Stop Sounds

Stop sounds are produced when we stop the flow of air from our mouth and then let it out in one short puff. If you put your palm in front of your mouth, you can feel the burst of air as you say the sounds: /p/ /b/ /t/ /d/ /k/ /g/. It is important to avoid adding the schwa sound (similar to /uh/) when we say these sounds. For instance, saying /buh/ instead of /b/ or /kuh/ instead of /k/. You will notice the consequences of this when you see a student spell the word *dog* like this: *duog*, Or you hear a beginning reader attempt to decode the word *bat* by blending the sounds /buh/ /ă/ /t/. It adds an extra level of difficulty to the process. Try to clip off the schwa sound. Additionally, it will help if you avoid using your vocal cords for sounds such as /p/, /k/, and /t/, which are unvoiced. If you use your voice on these sounds, it is probably because you are adding the schwa. More on voiced and unvoiced sounds on page 18.

Nasal Sounds

Nasal sounds are fun to demonstrate for students. Try this: say /m/. Now say the sound again, but this time plug your nose. You can't make the sound! That is because the air flows through our nose when we produce these sounds. You can also say the sound while lightly touching the sides of your nostrils and feeling them vibrate. There are three nasal sounds: /m/ /n/ and /ng/. The phoneme /ng/ is one sound that we make by pulling our tongue down and back. It is not /n/ (tongue up behind top teeth) and /g/ (back of the mouth). It can be difficult to isolate and pronounce, especially for young children, so some phonics programs will encourage teaching it in combination with an initial vowel: *ang*, *ing*, *ong*, *ung*.

Fricatives

When you hear the word *fricative*, think of the word *friction*. The tongue, lips, or teeth obstruct air as it flows out. You will feel friction as air is pushed out of a small space created by a part of the mouth that is blocked. As such, you will also feel vibration on your lips (e.g., /f/) or teeth (e.g., /z/). These are continuous sounds, meaning you can produce them for as long as you have the breath. The fricatives are /f/ /v/ /s/ /z/ /sh/ /zh/ /h/ and voiced and unvoiced /th/.

Affricates

Affricates are a combination of stops and fricatives—/ch/ and /j/. When you produce these sounds, you stop the air before releasing it. I think of a tug-a-war when I think of these sounds. The sound is pushing through a small space (like a fricative) and then suddenly lets go (like a stop).

Glides

Glides are sounds that are always followed by a vowel phoneme and literally glide right into that vowel (Moats, 2020)—/w/, /wh/, and /y/. Most American English speakers do not pronounce the unvoiced /wh/ phoneme and use the voiced sound /w/ instead.

Liquids

Liquids seem to float in the mouth (Moats, 2020)—/l/ and /r/—and their pronunciation changes slightly, depending on where the sound occurs in the word. For example, the /r/ in *read* is articulated differently than the /r/ in *fear*.

Some consonant sounds are voiced, meaning we use our vocal cords, and others are unvoiced, meaning we don't. If you look at the consonant chart, you will see the voiced/unvoiced pairs within the same cell, such as /f/ and /v/ or /t/ and /d/. Our mouths move the same way when making both sounds; however, we use our vocal cords for one but not the other. Understanding this concept will help you as you analyze students' writing. What do you notice if a student spells the word *spot* like this: *sbot*? Both /b/ and /p/ are a voiced/unvoiced pair. The only difference between these sounds is the use of our vocal cords. Teach this concept to your students by having them put their hand on their throat and notice which sounds they feel a vibration with (the voiced sounds) and which sounds they do not (the unvoiced sounds).

A couple years ago, I had a student who confused the letters *l* and *n*. Given that those two do not even look alike, I was so perplexed until I dug deeper into the consonant chart. Find the /l/ and /n/ phonemes on the chart. What do you notice? They are in the same column: "behind teeth." The place of articulation of the two sounds is very similar. As you pronounce each phoneme, you can see there is a very subtle difference between where the tongue is placed. I could then understand why my student was struggling with these two letters and subsequent sounds. Bringing attention to the difference in tongue placement was helpful to this student as I moved forward in my instruction.

Vowel Phonemes

One reason English is so complex is that it has 18 vowel phonemes with multiple ways to spell them. Unlike the consonant phonemes, there is no obstruction when we produce the vowel phonemes. They are all voiced.

I love the arrangement of the vowel phonemes on the chart on the next page, frequently referred to as the "vowel valley." When we articulate the sounds on the left side of the valley, our mouths tend to widen into small and large smiles. When we produce the sounds on the right side of the valley, our mouths make more rounded shapes. Additionally, as we go down the left slope, our chin drops lower and lower as we produce the sounds, dropping the lowest when we say the short /ŏ/ phoneme. Then as we go up the right slope, our chin lifts and our lips gradually close. The vowel valley is in the shape of a *V* to mimic this chin placement from high on the left to dropped low in the middle and then high again on the right.

Watch an explanation of the Vowel Valley.

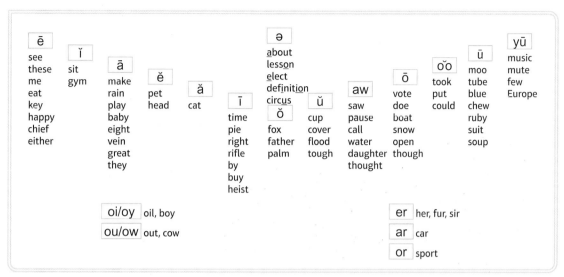

English Vowel Phonemes by Order of Articulation (Moats, 2020)

In the bottom-left corner of the chart are the diphthongs /oy/ and /ow/. Our mouth position shifts when we say those sounds, starting in one position and ending up in another. In the bottom-right corner are the *r*-controlled vowels—/er/, /ar/, /or/. In these sounds, the /r/ changes the sound of the vowel that precedes it. Our mouth is slightly more open and relaxed when we pronounce the vowel /er/ as compared to the consonant /r/, where the lips are more closed and rounded (Moats & Tolman, 2019).

The final sound is the schwa, a reduced vowel sound that often sounds like /uh/ or /ĭ/. It is often found in the unaccented syllable of a multisyllabic word. For example, think of the word *salad*. We emphasize the first syllable, /sal/, but not the second one, and we pronounce it with the schwa sound: /ǝd/.

Drawing attention to these consonant and vowel phonemes primes students for learning the corresponding graphemes (letters). Emphasizing the articulation of them helps students connect the phonemes and their graphemes. We help them to read and spell more accurately by teaching them the articulatory features of the sounds (Castiglioni-Spalten & Ehri, 2003; Boyer & Ehri, 2011). This doesn't mean we need to get super technical with students, but we can lead them into exploring what our lips, tongue, or teeth do when we produce the individual sounds. Additionally, we can provide explicit instruction in blending and segmenting phonemes, along with plenty of practice. So, when a child correctly identifies the sounds in a word such as *dog*, /d/ /ŏ/ /g/, he or she is much more likely to look up at you and say *dog*, not *horse*!

Instructional Implications

The value of phonemic awareness is clear. Now, let's explore some instructional implications.

Terms to Know

Onset: The sounds that come before the vowel in a syllable

Rime: The vowel plus the consonants that follow in a syllable

Onset	Rime
c	up
gl	ad
str	ict

Body: Everything up to and including the vowel sound in a syllable

Coda: Any consonants after the vowel sound in a syllable

Body	Coda
cu	p
gla	d
stri	ct

How Much Daily Time to Devote?

Phonemic awareness is best taught in short and frequent sessions. The National Reading Panel (2000) found that, during the kindergarten year, a total of 18 hours of phonemic awareness instruction provided maximum results, which ends up being about 30 minutes a week, or just six minutes a day. That said, a common pitfall is spending too much time on oral-only phonemic awareness. I've seen teachers spend 20, even 30, minutes on it a day, but this is *not* supported by the research. Additionally, the National Reading Panel found that focusing on one or two phonemic awareness tasks at a time is more effective than three or more. So, by maintaining a brisk pace and focusing on two tasks at a time, we can teach phonemic awareness daily in the amount of time research recommends.

Where to Begin: At the Phoneme Level or With Larger Units of Speech?

There is some disagreement among researchers about the role of phonological awareness activities in preparing students for the higher skill of phonemic awareness. Many children become aware of larger linguistic units, such as words and syllables, before they become aware of smaller ones (Fowler, 1991). To some researchers, syllable awareness seems to be a necessary immediate step after word/sentence awareness, on the way to phonemic awareness (Snider, 1995).

Onsets and rimes seem to be an intermediate step between syllable awareness and phoneme awareness (Treiman & Zukowski, 1991).

However, there is a growing body of research that points to the value of bypassing instruction in phonological sensitivity (the awareness of the larger units of speech in spoken sounds such as onsets, rimes, syllables, and whole words) in kindergarten, and beginning at the phoneme level (Brady, 2020; Blachman et al., 1999). Brady (2020) criticizes programs that require teachers to spend large amounts of time on phonological sensitivity activities in kindergarten and suggests limiting those activities to preschool. She argues that too much time is spent on developing phonological sensitivity skills and that those skills do not lead to phonemic awareness. Since phoneme-level skills directly support reading and spelling, they should be given priority.

Begin with two-phoneme words (e.g., *be*, *at*) before moving on to three-phoneme words (e.g., *chat*, *sun*), four-phoneme words (e.g., *flag*, *rest*), and five-phoneme words (e.g., *plump*, *strap*). Additionally, note that students develop an awareness of the external phonemes (e.g., /f/ in *fan*; /p/ in *top*) before the internal phonemes (e.g., /i/ in *kid*; /l/ in *sleep*; /s/ in *task*).

I can see so much value in getting to the phoneme level as quickly as possible. However, I believe *some* students *do* need more practice with the larger units before moving on to the phonemes. When I taught kindergarten and had students who couldn't blend three phonemes, such as /m/ /ă/ /t/ (*mat*), I would have given them practice with the larger units. Specifically, I might have given them practice with onset-rime: /m/ /at/. If they struggled with that, perhaps body-coda: /ma/ /t/. If they struggled with that, perhaps syllables and asked them to blend: *ap-ple*. If they struggled with that, perhaps compound words: *bath tub*. This seemed to prime students for the more difficult task of blending individual phonemes. At the same time, until very recently, I never considered backing up to the two-phoneme level instead of working with the larger units. It is such an interesting idea, and I am currently exploring it with my first graders.

In summary, it seems best to focus our efforts on phoneme-level instruction in grades K–2 and practice phonological sensitivity instruction in pre-K and, perhaps for those who need it, in small groups.

Max, Part 1

My student Max started the year with weak phonological sensitivity. He was unable to blend simple two-phoneme words, such as *at*, *so*, and *am*. To complicate matters, this young student already felt defeated from his struggle with foundational skills in kindergarten. He came to me filled with challenging behaviors and self-doubt. Can you imagine? Even as a first grader, he had practically given up and didn't even want to try. As he struggled to blend two phonemes, I knew I had to back up to help him feel successful and better prepare him for work at the phoneme level. So, in one session, I had him blend the two parts of a compound word, *cup cake*, and praised him instantly. He felt success and with that success came a little bit of motivation. From there, I gave him two syllables of a word that was not a compound word: *pur ple*. Again, he was able to complete this task and felt even more success, and his motivation continued to grow. Next, I gave him the body-coda of a word: *ma p*. This task was much more difficult for him, but as I slowly and repeatedly stretched out the sounds, he was eventually able to blend them. When I, again, gave him a two-phoneme word, he was still unable to blend the sounds. I moved back to the body-coda of three-phoneme words and he was more successful. Perhaps three-phoneme words were easier for him to blend because he could attach meaning to them more readily. After all, many two-phoneme words are abstract (e.g., *the*, *to*, *in*); three-phoneme words tend to be less so (*cat*, *sun*, *bed*). So, it's possible that when I said the body-coda *su n*, he could more easily blend and recognize the word *sun* because he could recall a mental image of the word. I repeated this process for several more lessons and soon he was able to blend all three phonemes of a CVC word.

As we were working on blending phonemes, we also practiced segmenting sounds in a word. Initially focusing on identifying the first sound of the word (e.g., say the first sound in *mop*), then identifying the last sound of a word (e.g., say the last sound in *fog*), then focusing on all three sounds of a CVC word (e.g., say all the sounds in *sip*), then work with four sounds (e.g., say all the sounds in *frog*) and so on. Note, I didn't withhold work at the phoneme level while we worked on those larger units.

How Best to Teach Phonemic Awareness: With or Without Letters?

Recently, there has been a lot of animated discussion about whether phonemic awareness should be taught with or without alphabet letters. Without question, children *do* need to connect phonemes to letters at some point, but the question is, when? Certainly, students who do not know their letters will benefit from oral-only instruction in phonemic awareness. But is oral-only instruction beneficial to students who *do* know their letters? There is certainly no harm in doing oral-only phonemic awareness, but is it the most efficient way to teach it? The National Reading Panel (2000) states that manipulating letters during phonemic awareness instruction is more powerful for improving reading outcomes than instruction that is strictly oral. Critics of oral-only instruction claim that adding letters keeps the task more specific to reading instruction since ultimately, students will need to use phonemic awareness to decode and encode words. However, in a 2022 webinar, Louisa Moats stated that many of the phonemic awareness studies included in the NRP's analyses used oral-only instruction and/or manipulatives at first and then linked the instruction to letters. She went on to say that using letters can actually confuse children if the goal is phonemic awareness.

I currently do practice oral-only, phoneme-level instruction with my first graders during whole-group time, and the sessions are brief (about three minutes), which serve as a great warm-up to my explicit phonics lessons. I devoted a similar amount of time to phonemic awareness instruction when I taught second grade. When I taught kindergarten, my sessions were closer to five minutes.

While phonemic awareness improves phonics skills, phonics can improve phonemic awareness skills. The relationship is reciprocal (Lane & Pullen, 2004). So, be intentional about integrating phonemic awareness into your phonics instruction. For example, while students are spelling the word *mat* with magnetic letters, you can break the word apart and show students how to segment each sound. See other ways to intentionally combine phonics and phonemic awareness in the "Strategies for Success" section.

Max, Part 2

As I mentioned earlier, my student Max came to me with weak phonological awareness and alphabet knowledge. In fact, he did not know any letter names or sounds. As he steadily began to learn his letters, we also practiced blending small words. He looked at the first letter and struggled to recall the sound. After some time, he'd say the sound and then go to the next letter and, again, struggled to retrieve the sound from memory. The next step was to blend the sounds together which, again, took a toll on him. Each of those tasks was momentous and required a lot of mental effort. Additionally, because his letter-sound retrieval was not yet automatic, he did not get very much practice with blending phonemes because it took so long. So, I covered the letters with my hands and gave him some oral-only phonemic awareness tasks (backing up to larger units initially) to help prepare him for the task of decoding the words by looking at the letters. For example, I'd say, "Max, let's play a game. I'm going to say some sounds and I want you to put them together to make a word. Ready? /s/ /ă/ /t/ (*sat*); /f/ /ŭ/ /n/ (*fun*); /l/ /ĭ/ /p/ (*lip*); /r/ /ĕ/ /d/ (*red*)."

It appears that, at times, oral-only instruction can reduce the cognitive load because students needn't worry about the letters. It prepares them for the more complicated task of adding letters. Max was able to practice blending five different words (without letters) in the same amount of time it took to blend one word with letters. Because he struggled with phonemic awareness, it was essential for him to have plenty of opportunities to practice this skill, and doing some oral-only PA provided this additional practice for him. After this oral-only practice, we went right back to the text and practiced blending again, but this time with letters.

On the other hand, once students know their letters and are asked to do more difficult phonemic awareness tasks, such as manipulation, using letters can help reduce the cognitive load of remembering all phonemes in a word. For example, I might ask a student to say the word *best* and then change the /s/ to /l/. It can be a challenge for them to recall the orders of all the phonemes and using letters might help them complete this task successfully.

In summary, there are many things to consider when it comes to the value of phonemic awareness instruction with and without letters. There's no question that it is essential to show students how phonemes connect to the letters that represent them, but perhaps there is more research needed about the best time to do that. If you do choose to do some oral-only phonemic awareness, remember to keep the sessions brief and focus on getting to the phoneme level. Additionally, ensure you integrate phonemic awareness with your phonics instruction.

I continually keep an eye out for strong research that will help me refine the things I do in the classroom. What I've said thus far reflect my current beliefs about phonemic awareness, and I need to be open to the possibility of stronger evidence coming out that might sway me one way or the other. Science is not stagnant, and there is always more to learn. It's exciting when our teaching becomes more effective the more we learn and the more we apply what we learn in our classroom.

Dyslexia and Phonemic Awareness

It's important to note that a hallmark sign of dyslexia is poor phonemic awareness. This doesn't mean that every child who struggles with phonemic awareness has dyslexia, but if you have a student with dyslexia there's a good chance she or he will have difficulties identifying, blending, and separating phonemes. A popular myth is that dyslexia is a vision problem, where the person "sees things backwards." Dyslexia is not a vision problem. It is a language-based learning disability. Please review one of the most commonly used definitions of dyslexia:

"Dyslexia is a specific learning disability that is neurobiological in origin. It is characterized by difficulties with accurate and/or fluent word recognition and by poor spelling and decoding abilities. These difficulties typically result from a deficit in the phonological component of language that is often unexpected in relation to other cognitive abilities and the provision of effective classroom instruction. Secondary consequences may include problems with reading comprehension and reduced reading experience that can impede growth of vocabulary and background knowledge" (International Dyslexia Association, 2014).

Providing intentional phonemic awareness instruction is important for all students, but especially for those with dyslexia. Those students will likely benefit from extra attention and practice in this area.

Strategies for Success

Here are some of my favorite strategies for teaching phonemic awareness.

Sing a Blending Song

Singing a song is a fun way to start off phonemic awareness practice. Before we start blending phonemes into words, my students and I often sing "Slide, Slide, Slippity Slide" (The Kindergarten Readers, 2017).

Watch a video of "Slide, Slide, Slippity Slide."

Then I give the phonemes in a word, and students blend them. For example, I might say "/p/ /ă/ /n/" and the students glide the sounds together and say *pan*, while gliding their hands down an imaginary slide. I continue to give students more phonemes to glide together into words.

Syllable Structure	Word Example
V	I
CV	me
VC	ice
VCC	ask
CVC	sack
CCV	ski
CCVC	skin
CVCC	cans
CCVCC	stops
CCCVC	scream
CCCVCC	streets
CCVCCC	stilts
CCCVCCC	scrimped

(Moats, 2020)

From there, I suggest gradually introducing more complex words. For example, you might start with two- or three-phoneme words with continuous sounds (e.g., *sun*, *man*) before moving onto words with stop sounds. Continuous sounds are sounds that can be easily extended or stretched out and, as such, are easiest for a student to blend. These sounds include /m/ /s/ /f/ /n/ /r/ /l/ /v/ /z/. Then move on to four-phoneme words with initial consonant clusters (e.g., *snap*, *black*). Then move to four-phoneme words with ending consonant clusters (e.g., *bunch*, *desk*). Then move to five-phoneme words with consonant clusters at the beginning and end (e.g., *stamp*) and, from there, move to words with three consonants at the beginning (e.g., *strike*).

Moats (2020) describes syllables as either simple (has a vowel with a single consonant before and/or after it) or complex (has two or more consonant clusters before and/or after the vowel). She shares the combinations of consonant (C) phonemes or vowel (V) phonemes in progression from most simple to complex (see the chart at left). Note that these structures refer to sounds, not letters. So while *ice* has three letters, for example, it only has 2 phonemes: /ī/ /s/.

Sing a Segmenting Song

I love to start our segmenting practice with the "Break It Down" song by Erica Allen-Jamison. Here are the lyrics:

Watch my students doing "Break It Down."

> Break it down, break it down; (Snap in between the phrases)
>
> Break it down, break it down, break it down. (Said more quickly, arms crossing and tapping legs)
>
> I say the words (point to self), you say the sounds (point to students).
>
> Break it down. (Arms crossing and tapping legs)

Then I say a word such as *fun*, and my students segment it (/f/ /ŭ/ /n/). I continue to give students words to segment.

From there, I suggest gradually introducing more complex words. See "Blending Song" on page 26 for a suggested progression of word/syllable complexity.

Use Manipulatives

Watch how manipulatives can support phonemic awareness.

When a student is struggling with a phonemic awareness task, use manipulatives to help them. My students love using mini-slinkies to help stretch out a word. Sound boxes with bingo chips or tracks with race cars are all fun ways to help students segment the sounds in a word. Pop It fidget toys can also be an engaging way to practice segmenting tasks. I most often simply grab some nearby Unifix cubes to help demonstrate a phonemic awareness activity. The goal is to eventually pull away from manipulatives, and for students to be able to segment, blend, and manipulate sounds in words without them. Consider them a temporary scaffold.

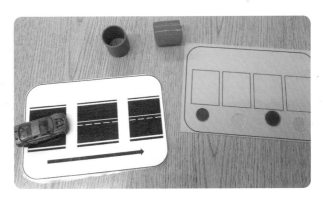

Whenever I introduce a new level of difficulty to a student, such as going from segmenting CVC words (e.g., *sap*) to words with initial consonant clusters (e.g., *slap*), I almost always pull out a manipulative. After a few lessons, I can usually put the manipulative away because the student no longer needs it to carry out the task. Once the student can do the task easily in a couple of seconds, I move her or him onto something more difficult, and the manipulatives come out again.

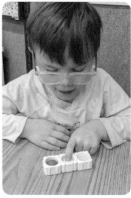

Focus on Articulation

Focusing on how we articulate sounds can be a huge help to students. When students are struggling to segment sounds, direct them to the mouth movement changes. Each change in mouth movement makes a separate sound. Students can count the number of mouth movement changes as the teacher models segmenting in order to help them become aware of how to hear and how to feel different sounds in words.

When writing, each new mouth movement cues us to write another grapheme. For example, if your student spells the word *sad* "sd," direct their attention to your mouth as you say the word *sad*. Show how your chin lowers in the middle of this word. Also point out that the chin does not lower in the sounds /s/ and /d/. Point to your chin as you slowly pronounce *sad* and help her identify the missing sound /ă/. You could also give her a small mirror so she can watch her own mouth articulate the sounds. This is especially helpful with phonemes that are easily confused for young students. Many of my first graders are still learning to pronounce the unvoiced phoneme /th/ and often use /f/ instead. When my student spelled the word *bath* "baf," I had him use a mirror and look at the difference between these two sounds. I showed him how his tongue went between his teeth when he said /th/, and that his bottom lip went behind his top teeth when he said /f/. Even though the phonemes can sound similar, they are articulated very differently. Keep some small mirrors on hand so that students can use them when they need to.

Encourage Gestures

Using hand gestures is another way to keep students engaged and support them as they practice phonemic awareness tasks. These motions are especially useful in whole-group activities, when manipulatives aren't as feasible. There are many different options. Here are a couple that I use:

- Extend your right arm in front of you and use your left hand to tap the shoulder of your extended arm (for initial sound), elbow (for medial sound), and the hand (for final sound).
- Have students tap out the phonemes with their fingers and thumb, on the table, or on the palm of their other hand.

Gestures are a great way for students to actively participate during phonemic awareness tasks.

Create a Sound-Spelling Wall

My sound-spelling wall has provided so much clarity in the phoneme-grapheme correspondences that I teach. Using the term sound-spelling wall instead of sound wall helps my students and I remember the primary purpose of the wall: connecting the phonemes and graphemes. My wall serves as a reminder of

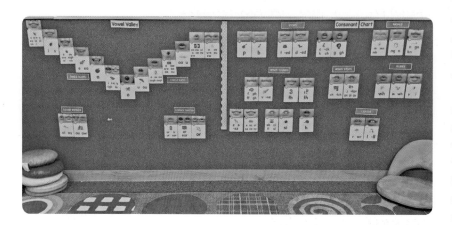

the critical role of phonemic awareness in learning to read and spell words. It helps me to be more intentional as I teach the various graphemes that represent individual speech sounds. It helps students develop an awareness of those sounds and how they connect to graphemes. Louisa Moats states, "Before children can learn phoneme-grapheme mapping for phonics and spelling, they need to be aware of the phonemes to which the symbols correspond" (2020).

Don't have a sound-spelling wall for the sake of having a sound-spelling wall! It's important to remember the purpose of the wall and your goal for using it: to help you nurture proficient readers and spellers. The wall is simply a tool to get you there. Although we currently don't have research on sound-spelling walls specifically, we do have research that informs good instruction. Instruction in phoneme and sound articulation leads to a solid understanding of phoneme-grapheme correspondences, which leads to reading words accurately and automatically, which leads to fluent and proficient reading. The "magic" doesn't come from the wall itself, but in the instruction.

Sometimes I "flip" my instruction by starting with the sound instead of the letter. For example, instead of thinking of letter-a-day in kindergarten, I think of sound-of-the-day. Here's an example:

> "Today we are talking about this sound: /f/. Can you say this sound with me? /f/ Let's get out our mirrors and see what our mouth is doing when we say this sound. Say /f/. What are your lips doing when you say this sound? Notice

how my bottom lip goes behind my top teeth. Watch /f/. Put your hand out in front of your mouth and say /f/. Do you feel the air blowing? Put your hand on your throat. Do we use our voice when we say this sound? Do you feel a vibration? Nope, there is no vibration, so we know that we do not use our voice when we say this sound. I'm going to say some words. If you hear the /f/ sound, show me a thumbs up. If you do not hear the /f/ sound, show me a thumbs down. Ready? *fish, chair, safe, puff, book, fin.* Nice job."

"Let's find this sound on our sound-spelling wall. Can you find the mouth picture for /f/? There it is! Let's find out what letter spells this sound. (Remove the sticky note that is covering the letter *f*.) It's the letter *f*! We will learn more about this letter today."

I can then move into my letter *f* instruction. The sound-spelling wall lessons serve as a bridge to my phonics lessons. I could use this same lesson in second grade, only I would focus on a different grapheme, such as *ph*, and words such as *graph* and *morph*.

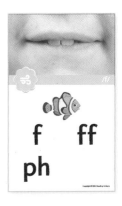

If you display a sound-spelling wall, make sure to cover the graphemes with sticky notes until you have explicitly taught them.

Students can refer to the wall as they write to provide spelling support. When I was teaching second grade, I had a student who struggled to remember the digraph *th* at the beginning of the year. I remember working with a small group of students as that little boy was sitting at his desk writing. He caught my attention with a quizzical expression, and I could see his tongue between his teeth as he produced the sound. I made the same movement with my mouth and pointed at it. Then I pointed at the corresponding mouth picture on our sound-spelling wall. He watched closely as I then pointed to the letters *th* beneath the picture. His face lit up because he understood clearly what I was showing him, and he quickly went back to writing, using the correct grapheme. The interaction only took a few seconds and didn't disrupt the group I was working with. And the boy knew exactly where to look the next time he needed help, and very soon he didn't need help at all.

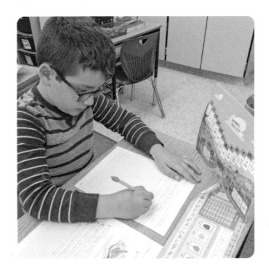

How to Create a Sound-Spelling Wall

A sound-spelling wall is simply a way to represent the different spellings of the 44 phonemes of English. It is a visual reminder to you and your students of your phonics instruction. You can purchase a premade sound-spelling wall, a digital version that you print, or even make your own. Check the ELA curriculum you have, because there may be grapheme cards included that you can use.

1. Find space. First decide where you have room to display the sound-spelling wall in your classroom. Whether it be under your windows or whiteboard, on a bulletin board or cabinets, choose a spot that students will be able to see easily.

2. Create some sort of division between the consonant and vowel phonemes.

3. Using Louisa Moats's vowel valley as a guide, set up your vowel grapheme cards in the same way.

4. If you have the room, set up the consonant grapheme cards according to Moats's consonant chart. If you don't have the space, group the consonant phonemes by *manner* of articulation (stop sounds together, fricatives together, etc.) only. Remember, the important thing is for your students to be able to find the sound they are looking for. Consider adding labels or pictures to help students find a particular group of sounds (a STOP sign by the stop sounds, a nose by the nasals, etc.).

5. Add mouth pictures. You can purchase these or make your own. Originally, I used my own children as models to create mouth pictures. It would also be fun to use your own students! If you dislike photographs of real mouths, consider using graphic representations.

6. Cover or turn over all spellings until you have taught them. It would be overwhelming for students to see all those graphemes at once! I cover each spelling with a sticky note and then reveal it as I teach it. That way, if some students are ready for a new spelling before their classmates are, I can let them take a "sneak peek."

Try Word Chains

Word chains are a great way to build phonemic awareness and phonics skills at the same time. Students solidify their letter-sound correspondences as they work on decoding and encoding. They engage in blending, segmenting, and manipulating with letters. It's such an excellent activity! Here's how it's done: Give students a word and ask them to change only one phoneme or grapheme at a time to create a new word. Here's an example:

> "Let's write the word *sat*. Say the sounds as you write." (Students say /s/ /ă/ /t/ as they write the letters in *sat*.)

> "Now, change the word *sat* to *pat*." (Students must determine which phoneme changed and then change the corresponding grapheme. If they are unsure, encourage them to point to the letters as they segment the sounds in *sat* and then point to them again as they segment the new word *pat*. Then ask which sound changed. Students change the *s* to *p*.)

> "Nice, now change *pat* to *pit*." (Students change the *a* to *i*.)

> "Great, now change *pit* to *pot*."

Continue on this way until students have written around 10–15 words. Alternatively, you can tell students which grapheme, or *letter(s)*, to change instead of which phoneme, or *sound*, giving them decoding practice. Here's an example:

> Have students write the letters *s, l, i, p*.

> "What word?" (Students blend the sounds and say *slip*.)

> "Good. Now change the *i* to *o*. What's the new word?" (*slop*)

> "Now change the *l* to a *t*. What's the word?" (*stop*)

Watch my students doing Word Chains.

Flip between these two approaches as you see fit. I have students use dry-erase boards for this activity, but you could also use sound boxes or letter tiles.

Use Dictation

Help students recognize the connection between the sounds they hear and the letters they see through dictation. It's a great way to integrate phonemic awareness and phonics. Just be sure to follow a scope and sequence of phonics skills when you choose words. (More on that in Move 2.) A routine for dictation helps to build students' confidence as they focus on the skill they are learning. In this routine, I say the word twice, and students repeat the word twice (Reading Horizons, 2019). Then we orally segment the sounds in the word while we tap a finger to each sound. From there, students spell the word while saying the sounds. Here's an example for teaching the digraph /sh/.

1. I say: "The word is *ship, ship.*"

2. Students repeat: *ship, ship.*

3. Students tap each sound with their thumb and fingers: /sh/ /ĭ/ /p/

4. I use the word in a sentence: "I saw a *ship* in the ocean."

5. I say: "Now say as you write the sounds in *ship.*"

6. Students spell the word while saying each sound. So, for *ship,* they would say /sh/ while writing the *s* and *h,* say /ĭ/ as they write the *i,* and /p/ as they write the *p.*

7. I circulate to give specific feedback to students as they write to ensure each one has spelled the word correctly. Then I choose one student to write the word on the board, which is motivating for the students and allows time for me to monitor responses.

If a child is having difficulty, feedback might look like this: "Let's look at your word. When I read what you wrote, I read *sh**e**p.* (As you say the word, point to the corresponding sounds in the word, emphasizing the /ĕ/ sound.) But we need the word *shi**p.* (Run your fingers under the word again, emphasizing the sound /ĭ/.) Which sound do we need to change? Right! Let's change that /ĕ/ to /ĭ/. Good!" It can also help to focus on your mouth placement by pointing to your mouth as you make the sounds to emphasize the difference between them.

Encourage Estimated Spelling

Many students who have difficulty with phonemic awareness try to avoid it at all costs. They are often overwhelmed by the process of spelling words because of the cognitive effort it takes to segment those words, listen to the sounds they hear, and then write the corresponding graphemes. Certainly, it is a momentous task! These students often rely on the teacher or assistant, and always ask someone to spell words for them. Too often we think we're helping our students write by giving them the correct spelling. But having students work through the process of estimated spelling is an important step. It allows them space to practice segmenting words into phonemes, and we do not want to deny them that practice. I tell my first graders that they are still learning how to spell words, and all I expect from them is their very best.

As I review students' writing, I analyze those words to determine if all phonemes are represented. This helps me know what each child needs to work on to strengthen her or his phonemic awareness development. Their writing, in other words, is a window into their minds as they draft. For example, if a student spells the word *dog* "dg," it tells me we need to do some work on hearing and identifying the medial vowel sound in CVC words. If a student spells the word *flip* "fip," it tells me that the child is proficient at hearing initial, medial, and final sounds in words, but struggles to hear internal consonants within consonant clusters. So, my next step is helping that child blend and segment CCVC words.

Encouraging estimated spelling does not mean that I don't teach spelling conventions. These estimated spellings are only temporary. I teach spelling explicitly, too, and correct students' spelling as necessary. *But I hold them accountable for only the spelling patterns that I have taught them*. If a kindergartner spells the word *back* "bak," I don't worry, because "bak" is completely acceptable and appropriate for them, given where they are developmentally. But, by the middle of first grade, I likely will have taught students that we almost always spell the /k/ sound -*ck* after a short vowel in a one-syllable word. So, I remind students of that fact when I see this in their writing and perhaps provide more practice in that skill in a small group.

In Closing, Remember...

Phonemic awareness is critical for students to become proficient readers. However, research is needed to inform the best way to teach it. It can be difficult when reading experts we trust take different sides—such as whether to use oral-only instruction or not. However, life in the classroom races forward. So we teachers often have to decide what to do. I listen to the debates closely and with great interest, and then make the best decision I can for my students. I continually monitor the impact of my teaching, as well as the latest research, as my busy schedule allows. Science is ever-evolving, and it requires us to keep our confidence in check and be open to the possibility that there may be more effective ways of doing things. As strong evidence emerges, we can and should refine our teaching—and grow as professionals.

- Phonemic awareness is a critical component of reading instruction.
- Phonemic awareness and letter knowledge are reliable predictors of future literacy performance.
- The most common source of reading difficulties is poor phonemic awareness.
- Phonemic awareness is the conscious awareness of phonemes (individual speech sounds) in spoken words.
- Blending and segmenting are the most critical phonemic awareness skills because they are necessary for reading and spelling.
- There are 44 phonemes of English, which can be categorized into vowel and consonant phonemes. We can discuss these phonemes by their place and manner of articulation.

KEEP	Teaching phonemic awareness.
STOP	Spending inordinate amounts of time on the larger units.
START	Getting to the phoneme level quickly.

- Students need to develop an awareness of individual phonemes and how they connect to graphemes, their written representations.
- Phonemic awareness is best taught in short and frequent sessions.
- We need to get to the phoneme level quickly.
- Students develop an awareness of the external units before the internal units.
- We can and should connect our phonemic awareness instruction with letters.
- Science continuously evolves, and so must we.

Teach Phonics Explicitly and Systematically

The role of phonics was downplayed in my undergraduate program, as well as in the training I received during my early years of teaching. I was taught that phonics instruction interferes with students' understanding of the text and that it should be a last resort, only to be used when contextual analysis fails. There was a belief that readers "do not need to recognize every word in a sentence or paragraph to understand the message the author intends to convey" (Eldredge, 1993). But research proves otherwise.

There was a belief that readers "do not need to recognize every word in a sentence or paragraph to understand the message the author intends to convey" (Eldredge, 1993). But research proves otherwise.

Many studies have examined the efficacy and effectiveness of explicit and systematic phonics. The findings of the National Reading Panel (2000) show that it yields stronger reading gains than nonsystematic or no phonics instruction and that it significantly improves children's word recognition, spelling, and reading comprehension. More recent research continues to show the benefits of explicit and systematic phonics instruction (Ehri, 2020). Brady states that the results of several studies "point to the superiority of systematic, synthetic methods of phonics instruction for attaining more advanced reading and spelling skills" (2020).

Children in England have shown huge growth in reading achievement since the country mandated systematic phonics in 2006. The Progress in International Reading Literacy Study (PIRLS), an international assessment that measures reading achievement at the fourth-grade level, showed that England's nine-year-olds are significantly better readers than their American, Australian, and Canadian counterparts (Department for Education, 2017). Why not teach in a way that benefits all the children in our class?

Phonics Explained

Even though explicit and systematic phonics was discouraged in my early years of teaching, my colleagues and I were encouraged to engage students in word-work activities. I had a phonics activity book and would spend time each day using material from it. While it included games that encouraged contextual guessing, such as "Be a Mind Reader" and "Guess the Covered Word," it also included a "making words" activity that I enjoyed implementing. (Read more about the problem with contextual guessing in Move 3.) For that activity, students use letter tiles to manipulate and create words. This is a wonderful word-chaining task that helps students grasp letter-sound correspondences, but there was no actual instruction to go along with it. There was no structured

Understanding the Code

There are approximately 44 sounds in English, but only 26 letters to represent those sounds. And do you know what's even more interesting? There are over 250 ways to spell those sounds! We need to teach students how to connect the sounds they hear to the print they see. Students need to learn that a sound in English can be represented by 1, 2, 3, or even 4 letters. Look at all the ways to spell the long-*a* sound below.

t	r	ai	n
m	a	ke	
s	t	ay	
g	r	ea	t
w	eigh		
th	ey		
v	ei	n	

Some phonics critics will use this fact as a reason to recommend whole-word memorization. They claim that English is unreliable and, therefore, a waste of our precious instructional time. However, despite all these spelling possibilities, English is more reliable than not. About 50 percent of all English words are regular, meaning they can be spelled accurately by letter-sound rules alone (e.g., *sat*, *stamp*), and another 36 percent can be spelled accurately except for one phoneme (e.g., *from*, *been*) (Hanna et al., 1966). More words could be considered regular if we take into account their meaning and origin. For example, *one* is from Old English and was originally pronounced as it still is in the related words: *alone, lone, only, lonely*. Moats (2020) suggests that only four percent of all English words in print today are truly irregular (e.g., *eye*, *of*). Systematic and explicit instruction in sounds and spellings is essential to help students crack the code.

lesson plan and no scope and sequence of skills to follow to systematically teach students how the English language "works." Written English is a code for spoken language. However, I was essentially shooting in the dark because I didn't understand the code myself. Now if you had asked me, I would have confidently told you that, yes, I was teaching phonics. But in reality, I didn't understand what good phonics instruction looked like.

Phonics is the system we use to teach the sound-symbol correspondences of the English language. This skill is necessary for recognizing words in the English writing system. It is just one component of effective reading instruction, along with phonemic awareness, fluency, vocabulary, and comprehension.

The charts that follow contain all the phonemes in English and many of the common graphemes that represent them.

Consonant Sounds/Spellings		
Phoneme	Common Graphemes	Examples
/p/	p	pan
/b/	b	big
/t/	t, -ed	tip, jumped
/d/	d, -ed	dog, called
/k/	c, k, ck	car, kit, sock
/g/	g	gate
/f/	f, ff, ph	friend, sniff, phone
/v/	v	van
unvoiced /th/	th	bath
voiced /th/	th	that
/sh/	sh, ti, ci	ship, motion, special
/zh/	s, si	usual, vision
/s/	s, c (ce, ci, cy), ss	store, ice, city, cyst, miss
/z/	z, s, zz	zoo, is, buzz
/h/	h, wh	house, who
/ch/	ch, tch	chat, watch
/j/	j, dge, g (ge, gi, gy)	jam, bridge, gem, engine, gym

Consonant Sounds/Spellings *continued*

Phoneme	Common Graphemes	Examples
/m/	m	mop
/n/	n, kn	nail, knot
/ng/	ng, n	rang, sink
/l/	l, ll	lake, fill
/r/	r, wr	red, write
*/wh/	wh	what
/w/	w, wh	with, whisker
/y/	y, i	yellow, view

*Most American English speakers do not pronounce the unvoiced /wh/ phoneme and use the voiced /w/ instead.

Vowel Sounds/Spellings

Phoneme	Common Graphemes	Examples
/ē/	e, ee, ea, y, ie, e-e, ey, ei	me, tree, sea, many, movie, these, money, neither
/ĭ/	i, y	tip, gym
/ā/	a, a-e, ai, ay, ea, ei, ey, eigh	table, late, plain, say, great, vein, they, sleigh
/ĕ/	e, ea	ten, bread
/ă/	a	sat
/ī/	i, i-e, y, ie, igh	wild, time, shy, tie, right
/ŏ/	o	not
/ŭ/	u, o, ou	fun, ton, cousin
/aw/	aw, au, a, ough	saw, author, ball, cough
/ō/	o, o-e, oa, oe, ow	open, note, road, toe, low
/oŏ/	u, oo	put, look
/oo/	u, oo, u-e, ue, ew, ui, ou	tuba, boot, flute, true, flew, fruit, soup
/yoo/	u, u-e, ue, ew	music, cube, cue, few
/oy/	oi, oy	soil, toy

Vowel Sounds/Spellings *continued*		
Phoneme	**Common Graphemes**	**Examples**
/ou/	ou, ow	loud, now
/er/	er, ur, ir	her, turn, bird
/ar/	ar	arm
/or/	or	for
/ə/	a, e, i, o, u	ago, open, easily, wagon, circus

What Exactly Does "Explicit" Mean?

Explicit instruction means providing precise directions for teaching letter-sound relationships (Armbruster et al., 2001). It is an effective and efficient method of instruction that leads to positive student outcomes. Archer and Hughes (2011) describe four main elements of explicit instruction: content, design, delivery, and practice. The teacher focuses on critical **content** and breaks it down into obtainable chunks for students. The **design** of lesson plans should be step-by-step and follow a gradual release of responsibility that Archer calls "I Do, We Do, You Do" (see details on the next page). The teacher **delivers** instruction at a brisk pace, while monitoring students, providing informative feedback, and giving students multiple opportunities to respond. Lastly, the teacher gives students meaningful and judicious **practice** opportunities.

"Explicit teaching of alphabetic decoding skills is helpful for all children, harmful for none, and critical for some."

—Catherine E. Snow and Connie Juel

The "I Do, We Do, You Do" approach can be used to structure a single lesson in one day or it can be spread out over a few days, depending on the complexity of the concept and the needs of your students. Be aware that it's easy to go straight from modeling (I Do) to independent practice (You Do), but resist that temptation. Guided practice (We Do) is one of the most critical steps in this model. Students need plenty of practice opportunities with specific and appropriate feedback from us. Make sure you allow enough guided practice for students to be confident when they try the skill on their own. Because the amount of "We Do" students need can vary greatly, some of them will benefit from more guided practice during small-group instruction.

The "I Do, We Do, You Do" Approach

The "I Do, We Do, You Do" approach is a practical way to put the gradual release of responsibility (Pearson & Gallagher, 1983) into action. Here's how it's done.

I Do: The teacher demonstrates the skill and explains what she is doing (Archer & Hughes, 2011). For example, "Today we are going to learn a new spelling for the sound /ee/. Watch my mouth as I make the sound /ee/. My lips widen into a smile. Can you make the sound /ee/? Good. Another way we can spell this sound is with the letters *ee*. Watch as I read these words that have *ee*…. Now watch as I write a word with *ee*."

We Do: The teacher guides students as they practice the skill, prompting them with directions, cues, and/or reminders (Archer & Hughes, 2011). For example, "Remember we learned a new spelling for the sound /ee/ today. Tell your neighbor what the new spelling is. (ee) Yes, so when you write the word *sheep*, use our new spelling. Ready? Say *sheep*. What are the sounds in *sheep*? /sh/ /ee/ /p/. Good. Now, let's say the sounds again as we write them /sh/ /ee/ /p/." The teacher walks around the room to monitor responses, and gradually fades out the support.

You Do: Students practice the skill on their own, without prompting, demonstrating what they know. This allows the teacher to check for understanding and determine if students have mastered the skill or need more practice. For example, "Now it's time to write some words on your own. Ready? *seed*; *feel*; *street*."

Additionally, consider the approach's three steps to be fluid. Allow yourself to go back and forth between steps within a single lesson. Don't be surprised if your lesson ends up more like "I do, we do, I do again, we do again, you do, we do again, you do again"! This is what we do as teachers, though, isn't it? We monitor our students carefully to determine if they understand what we have taught or if they need more help. To learn more, *Explicit Instruction: Effective and Efficient Teaching* by Archer and Hughes (2011) is an excellent book.

What Exactly Does "Systematic" Mean?

The National Reading Panel (2000) not only advocated for phonics instruction, but *systematic* phonics instruction. To understand what *systematic* phonics instruction is, I think it's helpful to understand what it is not. An approach that is not systematic or explicit, encourages us to teach phonics incidentally, only when an opportunity presents itself, such as when we teach a particular grapheme only when a child stumbles upon a word he doesn't know in a text. Another example would be expecting students to infer word knowledge on their own. For example, a child looks at a picture and reads the word *boat* on one page, and when he encounters the word *float* on the next page, the teacher expects him to transfer the information he gleaned from reading *boat* to the new word, *float*. The incidental approach assumes children are able to discover the code on their own. It leaves immense holes in children's understanding of sound-symbol correspondences. Certainly, some students will be able to crack the code without systematic instruction, but many more will be left stumbling along and will not become proficient readers without it.

A truly systematic approach to phonics means teaching all of the major letter-sound correspondences in a clear, sequential, well-thought-out order (NRP,

Habits of Teachers Who Practice Explicit and Systematic Phonics Instruction

What they do:

- Follow a clear sequence of phonics skills, progressing from simple to complex.
- Leave nothing to chance.
- Use a program that connects and unifies skills.
- Establish routines.
- Follow a step-by-step procedure.
- Gradually release responsibility using the "I Do, We Do, You Do" approach.
- Break down critical content into manageable chunks.

- Teach interactively, giving students frequent opportunities to respond.
- Give students meaningful and judicious practice opportunities.

What they don't do:

- Only teach concepts as they come up.
- Expect students to discover basic phonics concepts on their own.
- Work without a reliable scope and sequence.
- Work without established routines.
- Give phonics activities instead of providing solid instruction.

2000)—or a "scope and sequence"—to avoid creating major gaps in students' decoding skills and orthographic knowledge. Learning is never assumed, and instruction moves from simple to more complex concepts. Teachers often ask me which scope and sequence is best or which one aligns with the science of reading. There is no research that one sequence of skills is better than the other, or that one is more effective than the other. What is important is that your sequence goes from simple phonics concepts to more complex ones and that you teach high-frequency spellings before low-frequency spellings. For example, you will want to teach short-vowel spellings and CVC words (e.g., *can*, *kit*) before moving on to words with long-vowel spellings (e.g., *cane*, *kite*) or CCVC words (e.g., *plan*, *skit*). See two examples of a phonics scope and sequence on the next page, from the UFLI Foundations program and Scholastic's Ready4Reading program.

Let Go of "Letter of the Week"

Pacing is always important, especially when it comes to teaching young students the names, sounds, and symbols of alphabet letters. Research does not support teaching only one letter per week (Piasta & Wagner, 2010). Instead, consider teaching a letter per day and then allow students time to master its name, sounds, and symbols in multiple instructional cycles (Jones et al., 2012).

I've had success with a variety of scope and sequences. The order in which we teach 26 alphabet letters can be particularly complex because there are so many different (and valid) reasons for going in different directions. Some say that alphabetical order is the best because students are usually familiar with the ABC song and need to know the sequence of the letters. Others say to group letters by their form to develop handwriting skills. For example, teach *c*, *o*, *a*, *d*, *g*, and *q* together because they all start with the same curve stroke. Others prefer to start with letters with continuous sounds (i.e., *m*, *s*, *f*, *l*, and *n*) to help with blending; and still others prefer to start with the most common letters in words (i.e., *s*, *a*, *t*, *p*, *i*, and *n*) to get students reading as many words as possible, as soon as possible. After a few months, most kindergartners will have learned the majority of their letter names and sounds regardless of the order in which they were taught. It's easy to get caught up in the details, but know that when it comes to a sequence of skills, it's better to look at the overall picture, pinpoint what our students need, and go from there. Phonics concepts should start with the simple and move to the complex.

Scope & Sequence
All Concepts (K–2)

Alphabet
1. a
2. m
3. s
4. t
5. VC/CVC
6. p
7. f
8. i
9. n
10. CVC Review (a, i)
11. nasalized a (am, an)
12. o
13. d
14. c /k/
15. u
16. g
17. b
18. e
19. CVC Review (all)
20. -s at the end
21. s /z/
22. k
23. h
24. r part 1
25. r part 2
26. l part 1

27. l part 2, al
28. w
29. j
30. y
31. x
32. q/qu
33. v
34. z

Alphabet Review & Longer Words – CVC, CCVC, CVCC, CCVCC, -s
35. Short a
36. Short i
37. Short o
38. Short a, i, o Review
39. Short e
40. Short u
41. Short Vowels/CVC Review (all)

Digraphs
42. ff, ll, ss, zz
43. -all, -oll, -ull
44. ck
45. sh
46. voiced th

47. unvoiced th
48. ch
49. Digraphs Review 1
50. wh, ph
51. ng
52. nk
53. Digraphs Review 2; CCCVC

VCe
54. a_e
55. i_e
56. o_e
57. VCe Review 1; e_e
58. u_e
59. VCe Review 2 (all)
60. alternate c (c = /s/)
61. alternate g (g = /j/)
62. VCe Review 3; VCe exceptions

Reading Longer Words
63. -es
64. -ed
65. -ing
66. What is syllable; open vs closed

67. Closed/closed
68. Open/closed

Spelling Patterns at the End of Words
69. tch
70. dge
71. tch & dge Review
72. -ild, -old, -ind, -olt, -ost
73. y as long i
74. y as long e
75. -le
76. Ending Spelling Patterns Review

R-Controlled Vowels
77. ar
78. or, ore
79. ar, or, ore Review
80. er
81. ir, ur
82. er, ir, ur Review; wor
83. R-controlled Vowels Review

Long Vowel Teams
84. long a: ai, ay
85. long e: ee, ea, ey
86. long o: oa, ow, oe
87. long i: ie, igh
88. Vowel Teams Review

"Other" Vowel Teams
89. u (push), oo (book)
90. oo (moon)
91. ew, ui, ue (chew, fruit, blue)
92. Vowel Teams Review 2
93. au, aw, augh
94. ea /ĕ/, a /ŏ/

Diphthongs
95. oi, oy
96. ou, ow
97. Vowel Teams & Diphthongs Review

Silent Letters
98. kn, wr, mb

Suffixes and Prefixes
99. Concept of suffix; review -s/-es plural; introduce -s/-es tense
100. Suffixes: -er, -est
101. Suffix: -ly
102. Suffixes: -less, -ful
103. Concept of prefix; Prefix un-
104. Prefixes: pre-, re-

105. Prefix: dis-
106. Affixes Review 1

Suffix Spelling Changes
107. double consonants with -ed, -ing
108. double consonants with -er, -est
109. drop e
110. y to i

Low Frequency Spellings
111. /er/ = ar, or
112. /air/ = air, are, ear
113. /ear/ = ear
114. /ā/ = ea, ei, eigh, ey, aigh
115. /yū/ = ew, eu, ue, /ū/ = ou
116. ough = /aw/, /ō/
117. signal vowels and alternate c/g
118. ch = /sh/, /k/, gn, gh, silent t

Additional Affixes
119. -ion (sion, tion)
120. -ture
121. -er, -or (nouns); ist
122. -ish
123. -y
124. -ness
125. -ment
126. -able, -ible
127. bi-, tri-, uni-
128. Affixes Review 2

SCOPE AND SEQUENCE

The Ready4Reading Scope and Sequence was designed with and reviewed by our expert authors and advisors. It serves as the organizational backbone for all Ready4Reading materials. Ready4Reading includes systematic instruction, targeted practice, and application for each step of the scope and sequence. Consistent review and opportunities for assessment are woven in throughout system components. Word Study is integrated throughout (as noted with * in the list below).

Alphabet Knowledge

Letter Names, Shapes, and Sounds

Consonants and Short Vowels

m	b
s	l
t	f
Short a	Short o
p	j
c	Final x
Inflectional Ending -s*	k; Final -ck
n	Short i
d	g
r	v
Short i	w
h	Short u
Possessives With 's*	y
	qu (kw)
	z

Review: Consonant Blends

s-Blends
l-Blends
r-Blends

Review: Consonants and Short Vowels & Consonant Blends

Consonants and Short Vowels
Possessives*
Contractions With 's*
Single-Syllable Words With Open Long Vowels
Consonant Blends
Double Final Consonants
Final Consonant Blends
Inflectional Ending -ed*

Consonant Digraphs

Digraph sh
Digraph th
Inflectional Ending -ed*
Digraph ch
Digraph wh
Final Digraph ch, -tch
Final Digraph sh
Final Digraph th
Inflectional Ending -es*
Final Digraphs -ng, -nk
Inflectional Ending -ing*
Contractions With 'll (will) (he'll, she'll, we'll)

Long Vowels

Long Vowels With Final e
Soft c and Soft g
Final e Syllables*
Compound Words*
Two-Syllable Words (Closed Syllables)*
Long a (ai, ay)
Long e (ee, ea, ie)
Long i (ie, igh)
Long o (oa, ow)
Long u (ew, ue)
Vowel Team Syllables*
Long e (y, ey)
Long i (y)
Inflectional Endings With Spelling Changes: -y to i, Drop Final e*
Open and Closed Syllables (V/CV, VC/V)*
Contractions With n't (not)*

Complex Vowels

r-Controlled Vowels ar, or, ore
r-Controlled Vowels er, ir, ur
Suffixes -er, -ly*
r-Controlled Vowel Syllables*
Inflectional Endings With Spelling Changes: Double Final Consonant*
Variant Vowels Short oo (oo, u) and Long oo (u_e, oo, ue, ew)
Variant Vowel /ô/ (al, au, aw)
Contractions With would (-'d) and have (-'ve)*
Diphthongs oi, oy
Diphthongs ou, ow

More Word Study and Special Spellings

Silent Letters kn, wr, mb
Long Vowel Spelling Patterns -ild, -ind, -ol, -ost
Prefixes pre-, re-, de-

* Word Study

Besides having a clear sequence of skills, systematic also means logically connecting skills—what students have learned, are learning, and will learn. Instead of teaching a series of isolated lessons on separate skills, lessons should build on one another. Provide opportunities to review concepts you've taught your students. Put into place a system for teaching multisyllabic words. Make sure the process your students learned for decoding one-syllable words will assist them as they learn a process for decoding larger words.

Who Needs Phonics Instruction?

The National Reading Panel (2000) found that phonics facilitates reading acquisition for people of all ages. You are never too old to learn to read! The panel also found that phonics instruction's greatest impact is in Grades K and 1. However, additional research shows that second-grade students with weak reading skills improve when provided with code-focused instruction (Connor et al., 2007). Furthermore, research also shows that strong second-grade readers *also* benefit from phonics instructions. "Phonics instruction in second grade in teacher-managed classes resulted in reading performance several years above grade level" (Brady, 2020).

Phonics needs to be taught in upper grades, too, to students who have not mastered the code, including English learners who are still on their journey to becoming proficient in English. Consider focusing your instruction on spelling and morphology (including prefixes, roots, and suffixes) to reinforce knowledge of orthographic patterns of English. By continuing to teach spelling in the upper grades, you further your students' understanding of English spelling patterns, and that understanding facilitates vocabulary growth and word recognition speed (Treiman, 2017). Moats and Tolman (2019) recommend pairing spelling and phonics instruction in kindergarten and first grade, and separating them in second grade and above. This is because students will likely be able to apply complex phonics concepts more easily to their reading than to their spelling. Reading and spelling are two sides of the same coin. However, spelling requires retrieving the correct letter sequences from memory, which is more difficult than recognizing those sequences in print.

Terms to Know

Phoneme: the smallest unit of sound in our spoken language. The word *chip* has three phonemes: /ch/ /ĭ/ /p/.

Grapheme: A written letter or group of letters that represent a single speech sound (phoneme). In the word *chip*, *ch* is the grapheme for the sound /ch/.

Digraph: Two letters that represent one speech sound. The letter pairs *th*, *sh*, *ch*, and *ph* are all consonant digraphs.

Trigraph: Three letters that represent one speech sound. The letter trio *tch* is a trigraph that represents the sound /ch/.

Vowel Team: A combination of two, three, or four letters that represent a vowel sound. Common vowel teams include *ee*, *ea*, *ai*, *ay*, *oa*, and *ue*.

Diphthong: A sound formed by combining two vowel sounds in a single syllable. The letters *oy* in *boy* and *ou* in *loud* are examples of diphthongs.

Schwa: A reduced vowel sound, similar to /uh/ or short /ĭ/, that is often heard in an unstressed syllable. For example, in the word *salad*, we put stress on the first syllable *sal*, but not on the second syllable. In that second syllable is where we hear the schwa sound. We don't say /ăd/ we say /əd/.

Morpheme: A word's smallest unit of meaning. In the word *cat*, *cat* would be a morpheme. If we added the suffix *s* on the end to make *cats*, we would now have two morphemes: *cat* (a single animal) and *s* (more than one). That single *s* is a morpheme in this word because it has meaning.

Decoding: Applying letter-sound correspondences to figure out the pronunciation of a printed word.

What Exactly Do Students Need to Know to Be Prepared for and to Thrive During Phonics Instruction?

The first concept we need to help students understand is the alphabetic principle. The alphabetic principle is the insight that English uses graphemes to represent phonemes (Moats, 2020). Written English is a code for sounds, and those sounds can be represented by letters and groups of letters. That may seem intuitive, but many children need help understanding the alphabetic principle. Once they do, they will be on the road to reading.

Students also need to be able to identify the letters of the alphabet. Some educators discourage teaching letter names before letter sounds, but there is research that shows beginning readers' knowledge of letter names is a strong predictor of later reading success (Shanahan & Lonigan, 2010). When I taught kindergarten, I always taught letter names and letter sounds together with great success. I was excited to hear in a recent presentation by researcher Shayne Piasta (2022) that there is emerging evidence that teaching the letter names and letter sounds simultaneously is best.

Next, students need to learn a variety of phonics elements, including phoneme-grapheme correspondences, spelling patterns, syllables, and common morphemes.

Finally, students need to learn how to apply those elements to reading and spelling. Transferring their phonics knowledge to connected text is key! We must allow time for students to practice skills in context—to apply what they're learning to meaningful reading and writing.

Instructional Implications

Let's consider some ways to plan and teach phonics lessons more effectively.

Components of an Effective Phonics Lesson

In general, your phonics instruction should explicitly teach phoneme-grapheme correspondences, blending those phonemes and graphemes to read words, and offer practice opportunities to apply those skills. To do that effectively, your lessons should include several important components.

Drawing on inspiration from Moats (2020), you can see the components of my phonics lessons on the chart to the right.

You can change the order of many of the components, but be sure to teach all of them. In some phonics programs I've used, dictation came before word reading, and it was just as effective. Sometimes I prefer starting with a phonemic awareness warm-up, rather than a review and statement of goal and purpose, especially when I do not need to introduce a new phoneme. However, when I'm teaching a new phoneme using my sound-spelling wall, I like to teach phonemic awareness

Download blank template for planning phonics lessons.

right before I introduce the new phonics concept so that I can immediately connect it to the grapheme. Feel free to tweak the order of components so that the lesson structure works for you and the flow of your instruction.

Let's take a closer look at each component. How much time you spend on each one can vary depending on your students and the complexity of the skill you're teaching.

Phonics Lesson Plan
1. Review
2. State Goal and Purpose
3. Give Phonemic Awareness Warm-Up
4. Introduce New Concept
5. Read Words
6. Practice Dictation
7. Read Decodable Text
8. Close
Later in small groups
9. Provide Extended Practice
10. Read Connected Text (decodable or authentic)

Phonics Instruction Should Include

- Explicit lessons in phoneme-grapheme correspondences
- Explicit instruction in blending phonemes to read words
- Substantial practice opportunities to apply those skills

1. Review (3—5 minutes)

It's a good idea to review previous phonics concepts before diving into a new one. A good review is interactive and includes retrieval practice, a strategy that requires students to recall information—to pull knowledge out of their brain, instead of us cramming it in. A common mistake we teachers make is to quickly recap information from a previous lesson, but that doesn't require any effort on the students' part and, as such, ends up being ineffective. It also doesn't help us determine if students have learned the concept.

In my phonics reviews, I usually include a visual drill, blending drill, and auditory drill, which requires students to retrieve and engage. I also review any previously learned concepts that are necessary to understanding the new concept.

VISUAL DRILL

For this drill, I use about 25 to 30 grapheme cards—one grapheme per card that students have already learned. Students say the sound(s) the graphemes represent as I show each card. This is a quick drill, about 1 to 2 minutes. In fact, my kindergartners loved for me to time them for one minute to see how many graphemes they could recognize. In kindergarten, our grapheme deck mainly consisted of the alphabet letters and digraphs (*ch, sh, th*), but in second grade our deck was much more complex (e.g., *ai, oy, -tch*). When you are confident that all students have mastered a grapheme, take it out of your daily deck so you have room to add the more challenging graphemes as you teach them.

BLENDING DRILL

I use my blending board to give students practice in blending sounds and applying the skills I have taught them. I intentionally include graphemes for which students need extra practice. This serves as a great review. Read more about the blending board in Move 3, page 75. Alternatively, you could prepare a list of words for students to read and display it on your Smartboard or whiteboard.

AUDITORY DRILL

For an auditory drill, I say a sound, and students write all the graphemes they have learned for that sound, saying the sound as they write. This is great retrieval practice! For example, I say /ch/, and students say "/ch/; *c-h* spells /ch/" while they write it. If I say a sound that has multiple graphemes, they write and say all the ones they know. For example, with kindergartners, I may say /k/, and they say "/k/; *c* spells /k/; *k* spells /k/." In first grade, students would include another grapheme after I've taught it (e.g., "*c-k* spells /k/.").

You could have students write their responses on a dry-erase board. Or, if you're gathered on the carpet and dry-erase boards aren't accessible, have them use a finger to "write" the letters on the carpet. I have students who need extra help sit near me at the front. That way, I can watch closely and help them form the letters correctly. I like to repeat auditory drills during small-group instruction for

Watch me reviewing phonics with the Three-Part Drill.

students who need additional practice because I can more easily give feedback that ensures students are forming their letters correctly.

2. State Goal and Purpose (< 1 minute)

After your review, present the goal of the lesson. Make sure it is concise, clear, and student-friendly. For example: "Today we are going to learn another spelling for the sound /n/."

3. Give Phonemic Awareness Warm-Up (3–5 minutes)

Help students get ready for phonics by having them tune in to the sounds in spoken words. If you are teaching a new sound in the lesson, focus on the articulatory features of that sound. Start by exploring the sound of the phonics concept being taught before introducing the grapheme—or, as Louisa Moats puts it, "How much easier and more logical to teach children each sound, then anchor the sound to a grapheme (letter, letter group, or letter sequence) with a keyword mnemonic (1998)."

For example, you might start a lesson on the graphemes *oi* and *oy* by saying the following: "Listen to the sound /oy/. This is a fun sound to pronounce. Try it. /oy/ What are your lips doing when you say this sound? Notice how our lips start more rounded and together and then widen into a smile at the end. I am going to say some words. Give me a thumbs up if you hear the sound /oy/ and a thumbs down if you don't: *boy, toy, jump, joyful, noise, thumb, boat, coin*. Great job! Let's find out what letters spell the sound /oy/. We can find this sound on our sound-spelling wall. Let's uncover the spellings: *oi* and *oy*. These are the two spellings for this sound. We will practice reading and writing these spellings in our phonics lesson today."

4. Introduce the New Concept (3–5 minutes)

Clearly and concisely explain the new phoneme-grapheme correspondence or phonics concept you are teaching. Keep this section brief. For example, after introducing the phoneme /oy/ in the phonemic awareness portion of the lesson, you might show some words with these spellings and explain to students that they will *usually* see *oi* at the beginning and middle of a word or syllable, and that *oy* tends to be at the end of a word or syllable.

5. Read Words (5 minutes)

Lead students in reading words that contain the target phoneme-grapheme correspondence, using the "I Do, We Do, You Do" approach. First, display words on the Smartboard or whiteboard and model how to sound out one or two words. Then have students read the words chorally together. Give feedback when necessary. Finally, pass out lists of the words to students for them to read with a partner. (You might also do this after dictation, as preparation for the forthcoming Read Decodable Text step.) During this time, walk around, listen to students, and help them as needed.

6. Practice Dictation (5–10 minutes)

Have students practice writing words and sentences that contain the target phoneme-grapheme correspondence, along with a few words that contain correspondences you've taught previously, for review. In the fall of first grade, I typically have my students write about 5 words. A few months later, I have them write 6 or 7 words and one sentence, but that may vary depending on the complexity of the phonics skill and where they are in their development. Monitor your time, your pace, and your students as you determine the best number of words and sentences. I always ask my students to read their words and sentences after writing them to provide another opportunity to decode. For more on dictation, see page 34.

7. Read Decodable Text (5–10 minutes)

Have students practice applying the target skill by reading decodable sentences or a decodable passage. I ask my students to choral-read 2 or 3 sentences that I display using Google slides. Then I pass out a decodable text to students and give them one minute to identify and highlight the target phoneme-grapheme correspondence in the text (e.g., all the words with *sh*). Then we read the passage. Sometimes we choral-read the passage and other times my students read the passage with their partner. Sometimes we do both. For a more detailed routine, see page 86.

8. Close (2–3 minutes)

Just like the opening review, a good closing is interactive and includes retrieval practice. You should briefly review the critical content that you taught, as well as provide a preview of what you will teach in the next lesson.

> "Today we learned a new spelling for the /k/ sound. What two letters did we learn that spell this sound? *-ck* That's right. The letters *-ck* together spell the /k/ sound. What sound? /k/ Will you use this spelling at the beginning of a word or the end of a word? *End of a word*. Correct. Tell your partner when you will use this spelling at the end of a word. [Teacher monitors.] You will use this spelling in a one-syllable word, right after a short vowel. Listen to these words: *snake, snack*. Which word has a *-ck* spelling? *snack*. That's right. *Snack* would have a *-ck* spelling because /ă/ is a short vowel sound. Listen to two more words: *lick, like*. Which would be spelled with a *-ck*? *lick*. Nice! Tomorrow we will learn another spelling that we see at the end of a one-syllable word, right after a short vowel."

I like to teach the next two components at a separate time, generally when my students and I work in small groups.

9. Provide Extended Practice (3–5 minutes)

It's important for students to have multiple exposures to the target skill, as well as plenty of time to practice it. Small-group time is a wonderful time to offer this extended practice because you can give immediate feedback and vary the amount of repetition and instruction based on students' needs. I provide additional lists with words that contain the target skill for students to read aloud. I also provide additional dictation practice (see page 34), word chains (see page 33), and word sorts (see page 59).

10. Read Connected Text (10+ minutes)

Another great way for students to practice their phonics skills is by reading texts in small groups. Some students will need high-quality decodable texts, while others will be ready for authentic texts. Having the students read aloud during this time maximizes the practice opportunity for everyone. Read more about reading decodable texts in Move 4.

Strategies for Success

Here are some of my favorite strategies for teaching phonics.

Understand the Code

It is critical for us to have deep knowledge of the code—of how language works—in order to teach our students well. Research shows that teachers who hold that knowledge are more effective (Puliatte & Ehri, 2017; Moats & Foorman, 2003). Increasing your understanding of phonics will help you become a more efficacious and powerful teacher. I recommend the following books to deepen your content knowledge in English spelling and phonics.

- *Uncovering the Logic of English* by Denise Eide
- *Unlocking Literacy* by Marcia K. Henry
- *The ABC's and All Their Tricks* by Margaret M. Bishop
- *Spelling for Life* by Lyn Stone
- *Phonics from A to Z, Fourth Edition* by Wiley Blevins

Use a Systematic and Explicit Phonics Program

A critical first step is to find a systematic and explicit phonics program that will work for your students. While you could learn phonics concepts and then create lesson plans on your own, I don't recommend it! Speaking from experience, it is tedious and time-consuming to put something together yourself. Additionally, with a quality phonics program, you will deepen your knowledge of the code right along with your students. You will learn fun ways to make concepts stick. I remember being delighted when I came across the following rhyme in the Reading

What to Look for in a Phonics Program

Be sure the program:

- Is built on a solid foundation. Are the authors knowledgeable about the English language?

- Presents letter-sound relationships in a clearly defined sequence that starts with simple concepts and moves to complex concepts in a logical manner.

- Presents sound-spelling relationships for both consonant sounds and vowel sounds. Offers students substantial practice applying the letter-sound relationships as they read and write.

- Contains quality decodable texts so students can practice the skills they are learning.

- Helps you explicitly instruct students on how to connect letters and sounds.

- Contains lessons that follow the gradual release of responsibility model (see page 43 for details).

Check online for The Reading League's Curriculum Evaluation Guidelines.

Horizons Discovery program (2019) to help students know whether to use a *c* or *k* to spell the /k/ sound before a vowel: "*k* takes *i* and *e*, *c* takes the other three: *a*, *o*, and *u*." This is not something I could have come up with on my own. A phonics program will take care of some of the heavy lifting for you. Then you, as a professional, can adjust the lessons as needed for your students and do what you do best: teach!

There is no such thing as a perfect program, and *any* program can be poorly implemented. But if you have a strong phonics program combined with strong underlying knowledge, it is likely to yield positive results in the classroom.

Distribute Dry-Erase Boards

A mainstay in my phonics instruction is individual dry-erase boards for each student. It is such a great way for students to actively participate in a low-stakes way. It's easy to see student responses as I walk around and informally assess how they are doing. I am able to give students immediate feedback and help them quickly correct any errors.

I like to use 11" x 16" boards, which gives students plenty of space to write. Additionally, I prefer double-sided boards that are blank on one side and contain handwriting lines on the other.

I set up clear rules and procedures for using dry-erase boards. Students raise their hands when they are done writing their sentence, and I check it. Once I have okayed it, they draw a picture to match. This is so motivating for them and they love sharing their pictures with their neighbor at the end of the lesson. I think one of the reasons students look forward to phonics lessons is that they simply love using the dry-erase boards!

Establish a Dictation Routine

As mentioned earlier in this chapter, dictation is an essential part of a phonics lesson that incorporates phonemic awareness and phonics. A routine for dictation ensures students feel successful as they practice applying phonics concepts to their writing. With a routine, you'll spend less time on transitions and more time on what's really important: learning. Revisit the steps for dictation on page 34.

Make It Engaging

Some teachers say that phonics is boring. But it does not need to be! My students love phonics time because of the enthusiasm I bring to it. Some will say that it's "drill and kill." I love what Anita Archer says in response to this. She states, "We have no reported incidents of children dying of practice" (2019). She says we can change "drill and kill" to "drill and thrill" (Archer & Hughes, 2011). Think of ways to improve your lessons so that students remain on task and invested. What is your attitude about phonics time? If you are excited, your students will be excited. If you dislike teaching phonics, your students will pick up on that. Make sure to keep a brisk pace to help students remain engaged, on task, and interested.

> Phonics is not drill and kill.
> It is drill and skill.
> It can be drill and thrill!

One of the most important things we can do in the classroom, that has the biggest impact, is to increase student responses (Archer, 2022). We should give students multiple opportunities to respond throughout the lesson, which not only increases learning, but also reduces disruptive behaviors. Archer recommends aiming for 3–5 responses a minute to improve student engagement and learning outcomes.

There are many ways students can respond:

- verbal responses, such as structured choral responses, group discussions, and partner conversations
- written responses, such as word and sentence dictation
- physical responses, such as pointing to page elements, thumbs up/down, and facial expressions

Even though phonics lessons follow a consistent, predictable structure, there are ways to bring in fun and excitement. For example, when I teach that *q* and *u* together spell the sounds /kw/, I host a quick wedding for the letters *q* and *u*. It's silly, yes, but it gives students a memorable moment that helps them remember this particular phoneme-grapheme connection. Students learn that *q* and *u* must go hand-in-hand in order to represent the sounds /kw/.

Sometimes I switch up our blending board routine (see page 75) by having students hold the cards rather than displaying the cards on the blending board.

My students love to call the *e* in CVCe words "magic *e*." The magic *e* has the power to jump over one consonant and make the other vowel represent its name, or the long-vowel sound. In this photo, the student holding the magic *e* dons a magician's hat and wand.

To learn open and closed syllables, we make houses to demonstrate and practice the concept.

Find ways to bring fun into your lessons. Who says phonics has to be boring?

Create Word Lists

Students need plenty of exposure to and practice in phonics skills to develop automaticity. I create word lists that follow the graphemes students are learning in our phonics lessons. During our phonics lessons, students read those lists with a partner. I intentionally pair stronger readers with weaker ones. Partner A (the stronger reader) reads the list first while Partner B follows along with a finger. Then Partner B reads the words while Partner A follows along with a finger. I encourage readers to help their partner if she or he reads the word incorrectly. I walk around to monitor and provide help as needed. If both partners have read the list, they repeat the procedure until I say to stop. We spend a few minutes doing this and then go on with the lesson.

Attend to Word Meanings

While explicit vocabulary instruction is not the primary purpose of phonics lessons, I encourage you to attend to word meanings when the opportunity lends itself. A few years ago, I made a goal to attend to vocabulary more intentionally in my phonics lessons, in the dictation step. Here's how.

After students have written all the words, I have them go back and read them. Then I ask if they can come up with a sentence that uses 2 or 3 of the words. Students love this challenge, and they say their sentences to a partner while I walk around and listen. Then I choose a couple students to share their sentences with the class.

Another way we attend to meaning is by playing the eraser game, from the Reading Horizons Discovery program, after students have written all words on their dry-erase boards. This is a fun way to transition from dictation and to review skills. I say, "Point to the word that is a type of pen made out of a feather. [Students point to the word *quill*.] What word? *Quill*. That's right. Erase the word *quill*. Now point to a word that is the opposite of short. [Students point to the word *tall*.] What word? *Tall*. Yes. Erase the word *tall*." I continue by giving a clue for each word until students have erased all the words.

Do Word Sorts

Word sorts are a great way to review and solidify phonics skills. I learned how to better implement them from Nora Chahbazi, founder of the EBLI program. For example, after teaching students the many ways to spell the sound /k/ at the end of a word (-*k*, -*ke*, -*ck*, -*c*), I have them do a word sort to review and master those patterns. At the top of their dry-erase boards, I have students write those patterns and number each column:

Next, I say a word that ends with the sound /k/ (e.g., *cake*). Students think about which spelling it has. Then they hold up the number of fingers that matches the column it should go in (e.g., 2). Then we say *cake* as we write it on our boards.

I continue until we have collected several words under each spelling.

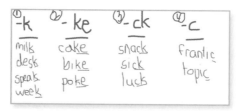

This exercise allows students to apply the phonics skills they are learning, as well as the spelling patterns. I might say, "Let's review how to tell which /k/ spelling to use at the end of the word. Look at the words on the board and see if you notice any patterns." Here's what they might say with my help:

- We use -*ke* if the /k/ sound comes right after a long vowel in a one-syllable word.
- We use -*ck* if the /k/ sound comes right after a short vowel in a one-syllable word.
- We use -*k* if the /k/ sound comes after a vowel team or is part of an ending consonant cluster.
- We often use -*c* if the /k/ sound is at the end of a word with more than one syllable.

I always ask students to read the words at the end of the lesson and we might even play the "eraser game" (see page 59) if we have time. For example, I might say, "Point to the word that has the sound /ă/? What word? (*snack*) Yes. Erase *snack*."

Try the "Vowel Intensive" Exercise

For students who struggle with short-vowel sounds, I implement a vowel intensive exercise that I learned from the Institute for Multisensory Education. First, create vowel tents by folding five index cards in half and labeling each side with the same vowel.

Each student sets these five tents in front of her- or himself in alphabetical order: *a, e, i, o, u*. Next, you say either a sound, syllable, or word, and students determine the vowel sound and hold it up. Here are some examples of how this exercise goes.

Sound Level

TEACHER: The sound is /ĕ/.

STUDENTS: /ĕ/. *e* spells /ĕ/. (Students hold up the letter *e* tent.)

TEACHER: The sound is /ĭ/.

STUDENTS: /ĭ/. *i* spells /ĭ/. (Students hold up the letter *i* tent.)

Syllable Level

TEACHER: The syllable is /ăck/.

STUDENTS: /ăck/. *a* spells /ă/. (Students hold up the letter *a* tent.)

TEACHER: The syllable is /ŏp/

STUDENTS: /ŏp/. *o* spells /ŏ/. (Students hold up the letter *o* tent.)

Watch the Vowel-Intensive exercise with my students.

Word Level

TEACHER: The word is *fun*.

STUDENTS: *fun. u* spells /ŭ/. (Students hold up the letter u tent.)

TEACHER: The word is *sip*.

STUDENTS: *sip. i* spells /ĭ/. (Students hold up the letter *i* tent.)

This is a great way for students to tune into individual vowel sounds and vowel sounds within words. I always start with the individual sound level and see how students are doing before moving on to the more challenging syllable and word levels.

Consider Multisensory Methods

Full disclosure: While I find value in multisensory methods, which involve the visual, auditory, and tactile-kinesthetic sensory systems, there is not a lot of solid research to support them. There have not been any controlled studies that compare instructional approaches with and without a multisensory component (Birsh, 2018). However, Berninger and Wolf (2015) assert that multisensory methods may make it easier for students to maintain their focus on instruction. We know that phonics instruction needs to be motivating and interesting in order to hold children's attention and to promote optimal learning (Ehri et al., 2001). For those reasons, there does not seem to be a risk in using multisensory approaches in phonics instruction.

I loved to bring in multisensory methods when I taught kindergarten. When students were learning letters of the alphabet, they used gel bags to practice letter formation, as well as to learn letter names and sounds. After I introduced the sound, letter, and formation of that letter, students went to their tables where I had laid out a gel bag for each of them, along with a practice page with the target letter printed on it. Students placed the gel bag on top of the page and use their finger to "write" the letter while saying its name and sound *at the same time*. It was such an engaging way for students to practice!

To make the gel bags, fill a plastic zipper bag with hair gel (I got mine from the dollar store), a couple of drops of food coloring, and a sprinkle of glitter. Next, get as much air out as possible before sealing the bag. Finally, duct-tape the sealed opening to ensure everything stays contained. I've had only one bag leak in my career and, thankfully, the student alerted me before it made a mess.

I also love to use sand trays during small-group instruction since it's easier to contain the sand, manage behaviors, and give immediate feedback. I set a tray of sand in front of each seated student. Then I give the group a sound, and students

▶ Watch my students using sand trays.

repeat it and spell the sound in the sand. Then they "shake out" the sand, and I give them another sound.

TEACHER: The sound is /p/.

STUDENTS: /p/. *p* spells /p/.

TEACHER: Shake it out.

Students shake the sand to erase what they just wrote.

TEACHER: The sound is /s/.

STUDENTS: /s/. *s* spells /s/.

I always have students write lowercase letters unless I instruct them otherwise since they are the letters they will see and use the most often as they read and write. The activity also provides great retrieval practice for students as they work to recall the letter(s) to spell a particular sound.

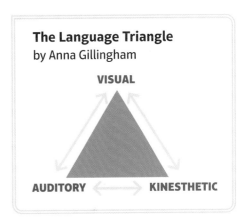

The Language Triangle
by Anna Gillingham

VISUAL

AUDITORY ←→ KINESTHETIC

Gillingham and Stillman (1997) explain that the goal of multisensory instruction is to help students build a link between the grapheme they see (visual), the phoneme they hear (auditory), what they feel in the mouth as they produce the sound, and the hand and fingers as they write (kinesthetic and tactile). So having the child state the sound of the letter while she writes it, even with paper and pencil, can also be considered a multisensory approach.

Try Explicit Phoneme-Grapheme Mapping

Help students apply the sounds they hear to the letters they see with a process called phoneme-grapheme mapping (Grace, 2005). This technique helps students realize that the number of sounds in a word may be different from the number of letters in it, strengthening sound-symbol correspondences so that orthographic mapping may take place. (For more on orthographic mapping, see page 70.) Students are given a word and then, in a grid, they write the grapheme for each phoneme (sound). It's important to remember that each box represents only one phoneme. This can be complicated initially, but the more you and your students practice, the better you'll get. Here are some simple steps to take to implement this activity.

1. State the word and use it in a sentence.

2. Ask students to segment the word orally.

3. Ask students to place a marker or dot in each box as they segment the word.

4. Ask students to write the letter or letter combinations (graphemes) in the corresponding boxes.

th	a	t	
f	l	o	ss
t	r	a	ck
q	u	a	ke
b	oi	l	
s	p	r	i	ng

Examples

Practice "Show What You Know"

One way to assess your students' phonics knowledge is through analyzing their writing. Implementing a weekly spelling assessment on Fridays can help you monitor your students' knowledge, as well as their ability to apply the phonics concepts you are teaching. I am not suggesting your typical spelling test, where students memorize a list of words. In fact, students won't be given the words ahead of time, but you *can* let them know the phonics skill that they will be asked to apply (for example, words with *-ng*). They will never be given a word with a spelling pattern that hasn't been taught. I call these assessments "Show What You Know." If students miss something, it tells me what skills I need to work on with that student and what to work on in small-group instruction.

If a large majority of my students struggle with a skill, it tells me I need to address it again during the whole-class instruction.

Download blank template for Show What You Know.

Offer a Secret Password

After I introduce a phonics skill, I provide reinforcement with a secret password. I write the new grapheme on a sticky note (e.g., *sh*) and place it on the doorway of our classroom. Every time students enter or exit the room, they touch the grapheme and say the sound (e.g., /sh/)—or the "secret password." Encouraging students to touch the grapheme ensures that their eyes are on the letters so, even if they repeat the sound their classmates say, they make a phoneme-grapheme connection. It's a fun way to get some extra practice in, and students love it.

In Closing, Remember...

- Research strongly supports explicit and systematic phonics.
- Using an incidental approach to phonics can leave students with gaping holes in their phonics knowledge.
- Systematic phonics relies on a clear and organized scope and sequence that progresses from simple to complex skills.
- Explicit instruction means precise directions and step-by-step procedures.
- Phonics lessons should follow an "I Do, We Do, You Do" approach.
- Allowing students to respond frequently during lessons keeps them engaged and enhances learning. It also reduces disruptive behavior.
- The sounds in English can be represented with 1–4 letters. Explicit instruction in those sounds and their spellings is essential to cracking the code.
- Teachers who have a deep understanding of the code are more effective in helping their students learn to read and spell.
- Phonics can be "drill and thrill"!

KEEP	Facilitating *effective* word work activities for practice of previously taught skills.
STOP	Using an incidental, haphazard approach to phonics.
START	Teaching phonics in a systematic and explicit way.

Teach Decoding Strategies, Not Cueing Strategies

I remember the parent of one of my students expressing concern that her child was using the pictures in books to read and not actually reading. I quickly responded, "Yes, that's what good readers do. They use the pictures to help them figure out the words." I was completely confident in my answer. After all, that is what I'd been taught in college and my early years of teaching. But years later, when I became a kindergarten teacher, I began to question that approach. I wanted my students to use the letter-sound correspondences they had learned to read words. When they relied on pictures, I felt they were getting the wrong idea of what reading actually is. They *looked* like they were reading. They *sounded* like they were reading...but they weren't.

One of the most impactful instructional moves I've made in my classroom has been to abandon the use of the three-cueing system. Three-cueing refers to the idea that readers use various cues to figure out words as they are reading: semantics (Does it make sense?), syntax (Does it sound right?), and grapho-phonemic or visual (Does it look right?). While the grapho-phonemic cue seems promising, it is often viewed as the least helpful of the three and to be used as a last resort when the other cues fail (Hempenstall, 2002; Weaver, 1988). You may not recognize the term "three cueing" but you are probably familiar with the "Beanie Baby Strategies," which are inspired by the three-cueing system. Animals, represented on posters or as actual Beanie Babies, with names such as "Lips the Fish," "Skippy the Frog," and "Eagle Eye," prompt students when they come to a word they don't know. Teachers may assist by saying things like, "Be like Eagle Eye and look at the picture. Does it give you a clue?" or "Be like Skippy the Frog and skip over the word." or "Look at the first letter and think what would make sense." There is no research to support these strategies. Let me say that again: no research! Are you surprised? I certainly was.

In fact, what the research *does* tell us is that these are strategies that *poor* readers use, *not* good readers. Good readers can read words in isolation, with

> When my students relied on pictures, I felt they were getting the wrong idea of what reading actually is. They *looked* like they were reading. They *sounded* like they were reading... but they weren't.

a high percentage of accuracy (Perfetti, 1995; Ehri, 2020). Weak readers tend to rely on context cues and pictures to read the words on the page. When we teach our students these strategies, we are literally teaching them to read like a poor reader.

There is some debate over who first came up with the theory behind the three-cueing system, but it is often attributed to Kenneth Goodman, a reading researcher. Goodman (1967) said, "Skill in reading involves not greater precision, but more accurate first guesses based on better sampling techniques, greater control over language structure, broadened experiences and increased conceptual development. As the child develops reading skill and speed, he uses increasingly fewer graphic cues." Goodman referred to reading as a "psycholinguistic guessing game." His theory spread like wildfire. Emily Hanford (2019) explains what happens next in her article, "At a Loss for Words": "These ideas soon became the foundation for how reading was taught in many schools. Goodman's three-cueing idea formed the theoretical basis of an approach known as 'whole language' that by the late 1980s had taken hold throughout America." Eventually, "balanced literacy" grew out of whole language, and advocates of it continued with the same debunked three-cueing beliefs (Adams, 1998; Hempenstall, 2006; Primary National Strategy, 2006).

"[Three cueing] is contrary to the scientific evidence on what works for the vast majority of kids and conflicts fundamentally with the recommendations arising from national inquiries in Australia, the UK and US into the teaching of reading."

—Caroline Bowen and Pamela Snow

When I taught my students to read using cueing strategies, I had no idea I was teaching them to guess. In fact, if someone had accused me of that I would have been offended. But when we take a step back and rethink what we are actually teaching our students when we ask things like, *What would make sense?* Or *Does the picture give you a clue?* You realize that, yes, we are actually teaching them to guess. We are asking them to take their eyes off an unfamiliar word to use context or a picture to help them figure it out. These are guessing strategies, not reading strategies. Context cues are great for understanding the meaning of a word or sentence, but not for decoding a word. Let me illustrate this point with an analogy.

When my two oldest boys were in swim lessons, I remember watching them, amused, as they'd literally walk back and forth along the width of the pool, making big swim strokes with their arms, exclaiming, "Look, Mom, we're swimming!" While other kids in the class were actually swimming, my boys weren't. They were walking. They were going through the motions of swimming, without actually swimming.

We see this often in classrooms. The students appear to be reading. Some even become quite expert at keeping up the appearance. Their arms are doing their strokes perfectly, but if you look under the water? They're only walking.

When we encourage students to use semantic, syntactic, and picture cues, we limit their ability to develop the skills they need to decode words. We teach them to use context clues and pictures to figure out words, rather than a deep understanding of how words work. We give our brand-new readers books that are written for the purpose of using cueing strategies. Once they memorize the book's pattern (e.g., "I like the..., "I like the...) and connect the picture to the unfamiliar word, they usually "read" that book effortlessly. But they are *walking* and not swimming. I don't want my students to walk. I want them to do the breaststroke, backstroke, and butterfly fearlessly. I want them to dive confidently into the deep end.

The reality is that not only are we depriving our students of essential skills, but we are also creating damaging habits that are difficult to break (Ehri, 2003; Tunmer et al., 2004). What happens when students are given more difficult texts that don't contain picture or context clues? What happens when their expert guessing skills no longer keep them afloat? They drown. When they hit third or fourth grade, and are given more challenging texts, their lack of skills becomes apparent.

It takes courage to look at our teaching and determine if it is effective for all students. The problem with the three-cueing system is that students often do appear to be reading the text. So unless we look deeply, we won't realize the child may not be decoding the words. Meanwhile, students are developing bad habits that get worse as time goes on, which, in turn, increases the time required for remediation. Dr. Linnea Ehri (2003) said, "...when phonics instruction is introduced after students have already acquired some reading skill, it may

Mia

ONE STUDENT'S STORY

I had a student, Mia, who struggled with reading. By the end of kindergarten, she knew only a handful of letters. I remember administering our state-mandated, end-of-year assessment. When I placed the required patterned book in front of her, she quickly scanned the words on the first page and then studied the picture. She looked up at me, clearly perplexed, and then looked back down and found the high-frequency word *I*. Then she looked at the picture again and said, "I see the dog." She turned the page and continued in the same fashion: "I see the ball," "I see the house," and so on. She "read" the whole book perfectly. But she knew only a few letters and barely any high-frequency words, so did she really read it or was she just an expert guesser? She certainly gave the appearance of reading.

be more difficult to step in and influence how they read, because it requires changing students' habits. For example, to improve their accuracy, students may need to suppress the habit of guessing words based on context and minimal letter cues, to slow down, and to examine spellings of words more fully when they read them. Findings suggest that using phonics instruction to remediate reading problems may be harder than using phonics at the earliest point to prevent reading difficulties."

We must abandon cueing strategies to ensure students are learning to read and not just going through the motions. Do not be afraid to look deeply into your instruction. Ask the hard questions, question the strategies you are teaching, and look at the research (or lack thereof) behind them. Are you teaching your students to swim?

Decoding Strategies/Orthographic Mapping Explained

We want our students to become familiar with the details of words, and cueing strategies pull students' attention away from those details. Students need to map the sounds they hear (phonemes) to the letters and letter combinations they see on the page (graphemes). When students take their eyes off the words to use cueing strategies, it inhibits their ability to store those words in their memory (Ehri, 2020). Ehri suggests *orthographic mapping* as a necessary process of reading development. In her words, orthographic mapping "involves the formation of letter-sound connections to bond the spellings, pronunciations, and meanings of specific words in memory (2013)." Students need to connect a word's phonemes to its graphemes, and attach them to meaning, so that the word is automatically recognized, or read by sight. Sargiani and colleagues said it best: "When readers apply their grapheme-phoneme knowledge to decode new words, connections are formed between graphemes in written words and phonemes in spoken words. This bonds the spellings of those words to their pronunciations and meanings and stores all of these identities together as lexical units in memory. Subsequently, when these words are seen, readers can read the words as single units from memory automatically by sight. Decoding letter by letter is no longer needed to read the words" (2021).

When students no longer need to sound out a word, and instead can recognize it instantly and effortlessly, they have orthographically mapped that word. They can read it by sight. To be clear: They have not memorized the word as a whole unit, and instead have become so familiar with the details of the word (the sound-spelling correspondences, the pronunciation, the meaning) that they can recognize it automatically. David Kilpatrick (2016) describes orthographic mapping as the "mental process we use to permanently store words for immediate, effortless retrieval." How long it will take for this to happen depends on the student. Some students may need many more opportunities to practice and apply new skills than other students.

> *"The best 'cue' to a word is the word itself."*
>
> —Mark Seidenberg

If your students have been taught the three-cueing system, they have most likely developed the bad habit of guessing. You will need to help them unlearn the old habits and teach them new ones.

Instructional Implications

Perhaps the best alternative to the three-cueing system is explicit instruction in phonemic awareness and phonics. Having a strong foundation in those essential areas will build students' decoding skills and prevent them from relying on context and picture cues to figure out words on a page. No cues are needed when you are explicitly teaching letter-sound relationships and using texts that allow students to practice their emerging decoding skills. Let Ehri's theory of orthographic mapping guide you as you teach those skills and help students when they come to an unknown word. Students need to connect the sounds they are saying to the print on the page. To do that well, they need to analyze the internal units of words, linking the spelling to the pronunciation and meaning in order for orthographic mapping to take place. Be sure to review Moves 1 and 2 for information on explicit, systematic instruction in phonemic awareness and phonics. Additionally, the kind of texts we choose for our novice readers have an enormous impact on students' ability to apply decoding strategies over cueing strategies. Move 4 discusses that in more depth.

Strategies for Success

So instead of using three-cueing strategies, how should we respond when students come to an unknown word? Here are some of my favorite ideas.

Error-Correction Procedure

1. **Pointing Prompt:** Point to the part of the word the student missed and allow time for him to state the correct sound.

2. **Verbal Prompt:** If he can't recall the sound, provide it for him.

3. **Blending Prompt:** Encourage him to blend the sounds. If he is unable to blend the sounds himself, model how to do it for him (and revisit Move 1 for ideas to strengthen his phonemic awareness).

Encourage Decoding

When students encounter an unfamiliar word while reading, direct their attention to each part of the word and encourage them to identify the sounds and blend them, instead of encouraging them to guess the word. Use a pencil to point to the first grapheme and say, "What sound?" Then point to the next one, "What sound?" and so on, and encourage students to blend the sounds continuously as they move through the word from left to right. Consider covering the final sound in CVC words to prompt students to blend the first two sounds together. Then unveil the final sound and have them add it on. For example, if a student encounters the word *sat*, cover the *t* with your finger. Point to the *s* as the student says /s/, and point to the *a* as the student says /ă/. Have the student blend both sounds /sa/. Lastly, reveal the letter *t* and ask the student to complete the word: *sat*. Research shows that using connected phonation (continuous blending) is more effective than segmented phonation for decoding unfamiliar words (Gonzalez-Frey & Ehri, 2020).

 Watch how to help a student with decoding when they come to a word they don't know.

Discourage Guessing

Give students the expectation of no guessing right from the beginning with the Decoding Dragon, a fiery character come to life by author and linguist Lyn Stone. She introduced the dragon on Twitter saying, "Announcing our newest, fiercest character: The Decoding Dragon! She chases the Guessing Monster away." Explain to students that when we guess, we are letting the Guessing Monster take over! We need to resist the urge to guess with the help of the Decoding Dragon. You might display a picture or even get a stuffed dragon to serve as a fun reminder to students to avoid guessing.

- Don't guess!
- Sound the word all the way through.
- Keep track with your finger.
- Break long words into syllables.

Lifelong Literacy

The Decoding Dragon keeps the Guessing Monster away!

To help break the guessing habit, play the Snowman Game (Stone, 2019). Each time a student guesses a word while reading, draw a part of your snowman. The student's goal is to prevent you from completing your snowman by decoding words rather than guessing them. Alternatively, draw the full snowman on the board and erase elements each time the student guesses rather than decodes. Let your student know that if they come to a word they don't know, they should say all the sounds in the word and that you will help them if they need help, but they should not guess.

Encourage Students to Keep Their Eyes on the Words

One of the most common behaviors of struggling readers is neglecting to keep their eyes on the words. They will look to us for approval or help, look at the ceiling, look at the picture for a clue, or look at almost anything else to avoid the words themselves. We want those students to develop the habit of keeping their eyes on the words the entire time they are reading. After all, how can they map those phonemes to graphemes if they don't look at the word? When one of my students takes her or his eyes off the word, I say, "Now look at the word while you say it." Even if the student reads the word correctly, I encourage rereading the word while looking at it to develop the habit—and, from there, I have the student reread the sentence that contains the word to further develop the habit.

▶ Watch what to do when a student guesses at words.

If a student looks up at me for help, I draw her attention back down, using a pencil. Then I encourage her to sound out the word (more on that below). If she looks up at me to confirm she read the word correctly, I draw her attention back to the word and have *her* check the word to confirm accuracy before telling her "yes." We want to help students become less dependent on us, and more confident in themselves.

I use a lot of positive reinforcement with students who struggle to keep their eyes on the words. For example, the first grader I'm currently tutoring earns "gems" (i.e., colorful plastic beads from the dollar store) if she focuses on the words in a sentence, paragraph, or entire page of the book we're reading. I'll put a couple in her treasure chest and say, "I love how you kept your eyes on the words." This motivates her to resist the urge to look away.

In my classroom, I don't use gems, but often award points by playing a game. In the corner of students' individual dry-erase boards, I create a T-chart and put a *T* for teacher at the top of the left column and the student's first initial at the top of the right. Each time the student reads without guessing or looking away, I put a tally mark in the right column. Each time the student takes her eyes off the words while reading, I put a mark in the left column. This serves as a quick reminder of what I'm looking for. At the end of the lesson, we see who has the most marks. I give students lots of opportunities to beat me to keep the game fun, while reinforcing the desired behavior.

Provide the Unknown Sound

If students encounter a word with an unfamiliar grapheme, tell them the grapheme's sound and then have them blend the word. For example, if a student comes to the word *house* but does not know that *ou* represents the sound /ow/, follow these steps:

1. Point to the letter *h* and ask the child to say the sound.
2. Point to the letters *ou* and say, "These letters spell /ow/. What sound?" and have the child repeat the sound.
3. Ask the child to blend the two sounds together, "how."
4. Point to the letters *se* as the child says /s/.
5. Encourage the child to blend the sounds and say the entire word: *house*.

Encourage Finger Tracking

To help students look carefully at the print, keep their place on the line and page, and focus on matching the letters to sounds, encourage them to point to words as they are reading them. Make sure the student's finger is under the word being read and not lagging behind or jumping ahead. I often tell students, "Be sure you are pointing to the word you're saying" or "Your finger should match your mouth." Sometimes I use a pencil to point above the words while the child points below them to assist her in keeping pace with me and keeping her finger exactly on the words being said.

Most of the time, I have students use their fingers to track the words, but occasionally I use witch's fingers (buy them at Halloween time), popsicle sticks, or even finger lights to keep things interesting.

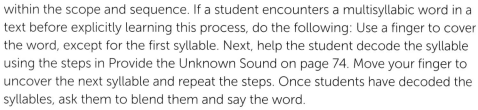

Break Long Words Into Syllables

Teach students a process for breaking words into syllables. Most phonics programs will teach a specific method for this within the scope and sequence. If a student encounters a multisyllabic word in a text before explicitly learning this process, do the following: Use a finger to cover the word, except for the first syllable. Next, help the student decode the syllable using the steps in Provide the Unknown Sound on page 74. Move your finger to uncover the next syllable and repeat the steps. Once students have decoded the syllables, ask them to blend them and say the word.

Use Blending Boards

I use a blending board to help students focus their attention on individual word parts. This activity requires students to read words in isolation, which is especially helpful to those who have a strong guessing habit. After all, there is no context from which to guess when reading a single word.

I use a physical blending board, but many teachers use digital versions. You will need a stack of grapheme cards to divide into three stacks: initial sounds, medial sounds, and final sounds. It's critical to place each grapheme in the correct stack—for example, *x* doesn't belong in the initial-sounds stack. Rather, it should go in the final-sounds stack. Make sure to include only graphemes that you have explicitly taught in your phonics lessons.

Spell a word with the cards, such as *run*, and place your hand above each letter to guide students in saying the sound the letter represents. From there, have them blend the sounds. Change one grapheme card—for example, change *run* to *ran*—and repeat the process with students. While nonsense words are best used for assessment, it's okay to use them occasionally in this drill, as well as real words—just be sure students can distinguish between the two. Have them give you a thumbs-up when it's a real word and a thumbs-down when it's a nonsense word. Nonsense-word reading aims to develop students' ability to decode single-syllable words quickly and accurately (Kilpatrick, 2016). If a student scoffs at the idea of reading nonsense words, tell them that many syllables in multisyllabic words are actually nonsense words, so practicing nonsense words will help them read multisyllabic words—or "big words." You could consider calling nonsense words "word parts" instead. This activity helps students realize that by changing just one letter, a completely new word can be created. It reinforces those letter-sound skills and blending.

want	went	what	when	west
went	when	what	west	want
what	west	want	when	went
when	want	west	went	what

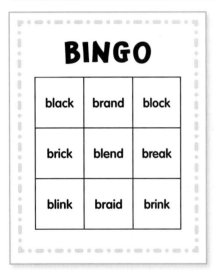

Download two blank versions of the BINGO card— one with write-on lines for students and one without.

Use Look-Alike Words

In *Equipped for Reading Success*, David Kilpatrick (2016) suggests using words that look alike to develop the mental habit of attending to every letter within a word. Use index cards or a word list that contain similar words such as *black, block, brick, brink, break, braid, blink, brand, bland,* and *blend.* You could create a word grid for students to read, like the example above, or even turn it into a Bingo game.

Fill in a blank Bingo board with look-alike words. When you call out a word, students search for the word and cover it with a Bingo chip. Using look-alike words for these activities forces students to look carefully at the internal units of the word. Cueing strategies will not work with this type of task.

Encourage Oral Encoding

When students decode a written word, they use letter-sound knowledge to pronounce that word. When students encode, they do just the opposite. They use their letter-sound knowledge to spell the word. Decoding and encoding require the same underlying processes, and instruction in one strengthens the other. Students who improve in spelling also improve in writing fluency and reading word-attack skills (Moats, 2005).

So give students many opportunities to spell words and encourage them to say the sounds in words as they write them to solidify sound-spelling correspondences. For example, students say /m/ /ŏ/ /p/ as they write the letters in *mop*. Remind students that their mouths should match the letter they're writing. In other words, they should make sure they're saying the sound *at the same time* they are writing the corresponding letter(s), and not slightly behind or ahead.

In Closing, Remember...

- When we teach cueing strategies, students can develop guessing habits that are difficult to break.
- The three-cueing system can create an appearance of reading, so look closely to see if students are actually decoding the words.
- When students take their eyes off the words and guess, it inhibits the processes necessary to store words in their memories.
- Orthographic mapping is the mental process we use to permanently store words for immediate, effortless retrieval (Kilpatrick, 2016).
- Students need to match the sounds they hear to the letters on the page to facilitate orthographic mapping.
- Students need to resist the urge to guess, keep their eyes on the words, and point to the words as they read.
- We can help students as they read by encouraging them to blend words continuously and break multisyllabic word into syllables, and by providing unknown sounds.
- We can use a blending board, look-alike words, and encoding practice to build students' decoding skills, as well as explicit phonics and phonemic awareness instruction.

KEEP — Assisting students when they come to an unfamiliar word.

STOP — Encouraging the use of pictures and context cues to decode words.

START — Emphasizing sound-spelling correspondences as students read words.

Use Decodable Texts Instead of Predictable Texts With Beginning Readers

Predictable texts are widely used with beginning readers. But I suggest replacing them with decodable texts. I'm not talking about beautiful, authentic books such as *The Napping House and Chicka Chicka Boom Boom*. I'm talking about those contrived, early readers with repetitive language such as, "We cleaned the garage. We cleaned the house. We cleaned the school" and so forth. Those books are written from the standpoint that reading is a natural process, and the best way to teach it is by encouraging students to memorize words and use pictures to identify words. But that is not how reading works. The only way for beginning readers to get through those texts is by memorizing the patterns or using the three-cueing strategies I discouraged in Move 3. But that is not reading! It is memorizing and guessing. It gives the illusion of reading but creates damaging habits that can be tough to break (Ehri, 2003; Tunmer et al., 2004).

Imagine you are a beginning reader and have been taught these sound-symbol correspondences.

◆ represents /a/	▲ represents /m/	● represents /s/	◉ represents /t/

Could you read the following sentence?

●◆▲ ●◆◉.

It took some effort, but I have no doubt you were able to read it: *Sam sat*. With practice and repetition, you would learn to recognize these sounds and symbols automatically.

Now, what if you had only learned the four sound-symbol correspondences above, and I gave you the following text:

♥ ●◆♣ ●◆▲ ◆◉ ◉◇+ ●◉✚✳+. ◇+ ✦◆● ♣♪/★☆✿ ✦◆☆✕√.

(*I saw Sam at the store. He was buying candy.*)

I imagine that felt pretty overwhelming. It seems almost comical when you consider it, and yet, students are constantly being expected to read texts they simply aren't prepared to read. We don't expect the same thing in other subject areas. For example, we don't give students a math worksheet filled with multiplication and division problems, right after a lesson on single-digit addition.

The first year I taught kindergarten was eye-opening. It was when I started growing uneasy about the reading methods I had been taught. After spending so much time on letter-sound instruction, I was excited to show my students how this new knowledge would help them learn to read. But the books we were given for them to read were predictable, repetitive, and filled with advanced phonics concepts that, as a kindergarten teacher, I had not taught. I felt as though I had to ask my students to throw everything they had been learning out the window. "Oh, this word you can't sound out." "Uh, look at the picture. Does it give you a clue?" I was so frustrated that they could not read these books without me providing their repetitive sentence patterns or instructing them to look at the pictures for clues— and that they weren't putting their letter-sound knowledge to use.

I had used predictable texts and cueing strategies when I taught second grade, years earlier. My students would read their books by using context clues and pictures, and thinking about what would make sense, as I instructed them to do. I would divide my class up by what guided reading "level" students seemed to be, but there was never really a clear distinction between the levels, and I was unsure of what *exactly* to do to help them get to the next level. As a result, we would just keep plodding away until we exhausted a level, and then move to the next one, hoping things would just click. I didn't realize that many students were

Kittens like to play.
These kittens play with a string.

Puppies like to play.
These puppies play with a ball.

A spread from a typical predictable text

really just memorizing patterns and becoming expert guessers. I felt like I was in a fog, and I didn't have any clarity into what students actually need to read proficiently.

The problem with predictable texts and cueing strategies never occurred to me until I started teaching kindergarten. I wanted my kindergarten students to practice their letter sounds. I wanted to show them how to put individual sounds together to make words. I wanted them to apply all the phonemic awareness and phonics knowledge they had gained. I wanted them to decode. Instead, I gave them a false idea of what reading was.

Of course, there are some students who will learn to read no matter what approach is used and no matter what texts are used. They will crack the code themselves and won't be negatively affected by these methods. That is why it can be easy to believe there is nothing wrong with predictable texts and three-cueing strategies. It works for some students, and it appears to work for others so it reinforces the debunked philosophy. But we must take a closer look, especially at how these students are doing a year or two after they have left the three-cueing classroom. The kindergarten teacher who was using pattern books may not have noticed a problem at all, since many students can easily memorize patterns and read pictures. It's the first-, second-, or even third-grade teacher who will discover that this child has become an expert guesser, but is unable to decode even the simplest CVC nonsense word. If a child cannot decode *cac* or *tus*, how will he or she read the word *cactus*?

Decodable Texts Explained

One instructional tool that we can use to help our beginning readers is decodable texts. So set aside those predictable books (typically guided reading levels A–D) and use decodable texts instead.

Decodable texts are designed to help students achieve mastery of the phonics skills they are learning. In a decodable text, the majority of the words are phonetically regular. In other words, they contain letter-sound correspondences that are consistent, and can be sounded out because they contain the phonics skills we've taught. Each text usually focuses on one new target skill. For example, the new skill might be the grapheme *ar* for the

> **Three Purposes of Decodable Texts**
>
> 1. Support readers in word identification.
>
> 2. Allow readers to apply what they've learned from your phonics lessons.
>
> 3. Direct readers' attention to the letters and sounds.
>
> (Mesmer, 2001)

A spread from a typical decodable text

sound /ar/, and the text would contain many words with that sound: *card*, *smart*, *far*, *jar*, etc.

The knowledge that the reader brings to the text determines whether it is decodable for them. It's important to remember that just because a text is called decodable, it doesn't mean it includes concepts that have been taught. For example, kindergartners who know all alphabet letter sounds, as well as the high-frequency word *the*, would most likely be able to read the sentence, "The pig sat in the mud." That sentence would be 100 percent decodable for those readers. However, consider the next sentence, "I ate a cake at the lake." Even though this sentence is phonetically regular, it would not be decodable for the kindergartener who has not been introduced to VCe words. The reader's knowledge matters. The decodable text we choose must be a good match for the reader, which means it must reflect the skills the reader knows. What is decodable for one student, might not be decodable for another. The more you understand about phonics concepts, the better you'll be able to use decodable texts.

Scope and Sequence Matters!

Not only do your students need decodable texts, but they also need these books to follow a sequence of skills that progresses from simple to more challenging. Stanislas Dehaene (2010) said, "At each step, the words and sentences introduced in class must only include graphemes and phonemes that have already been introduced." That is not possible if you have a series of decodable texts that's been assembled in a haphazard way. Choose a high-quality series that closely matches your phonics scope and sequence, starting with simple CVC words, moving to initial and ending consonant clusters, moving to vowel patterns, and so forth. That way, students can practice decoding skills incrementally, as you introduce new letters and sounds.

While you might want to use texts that contain high-frequency words or challenge words, be sure they don't contain too many. Additionally, not every creator of decodable books really understands their purpose or even what they are. Identifying high-quality decodable texts should become a priority.

Misconceptions of Decodable Texts

I am surprised by the controversy over the use of decodable texts, but I would much rather have my students blending and sounding out a decodable book than learning to look at a picture and guess the word in a predictable/repetitive text. After all, we should allow students time to practice the phonics skills they are learning, and decodable texts enable that. Linnea Ehri said, "Decodable books provide beginners with practice in applying the grapheme-phoneme relations that they have learned to decode words and to build their sight vocabularies" (2020). That said, let's explore some of the criticisms of decodable texts.

They're boring!

I have heard this complaint several times from teachers, but not from students. A couple weeks after I started using decodable books in my kindergarten classroom, I vividly remember one boy shouting, "Mrs. Kemeny! I AM ACTUALLY READING THE WORDS!" I wish you could have seen the look on his face. His joy and excitement were overflowing. In no way was he bored. Instead, he felt confident and successful because he had discovered a skill that he didn't even know he had. He had gained some phonics knowledge and now he was getting to put it into practice. No guessing needed.

Of course, I can always download and print texts, but I prefer having my students hold an actual book in their hands, and I have been amazed by the quality and artistry of some of those books. Contrary to popular opinion, many of them contain beautiful illustrations and meaningful stories that bring out all kinds of thoughts and feelings in my students. We discuss what's happening in the book and share our favorite parts. Small-group time with decodables is a favorite time for everyone. Any kind of text for beginning readers could be considered boring, especially for

This land has lots of wet mud! Frogs sit in mud.

In mud, the frogs' skin gets wet. Frogs will not get hot in mud.

the teacher, but I've never had one of my students tell me the decodable book they are reading is boring. Instead, they are experiencing the exhilarating feelings of validation and success.

They're so much harder!

It can be tedious to listen as a child slowly blends sounds to decode a word. You patiently listen as she carefully reads, "Ssssaaaaammmmm," and then you must listen as she sounds it out again and again on the following pages. It is easier and faster to encourage students to memorize a pattern or look at a picture and say the word that represents it. But if there is no effort, there are no results. That productive struggle is exactly what students need to cement letter-sound correspondences in their memory and orthographically map the word. That effort is evidence they are learning new skills. Reading shouldn't be easy at this beginning stage. So, yes, students will read slower at first, but they are making wonderful connections and, eventually, they will likely surpass those students who rely on memorization, pictures, and context cues.

The language is so contrived!

The language can sometimes feel stilted and inauthentic in decodable texts, but it's important to realize that the same can be said of predictable texts. But as new phonics skills are introduced in each book, the language becomes more natural quickly. I don't mind the occasional odd sentence because it discourages guessing and forces students to pay close attention to the words' details.

That said, I do admit that there are some very poorly written decodables but they are becoming rarer as the demand for high-quality decodables increases. Many have beautiful language, cultural relevance, and engaging storylines. If you have been turned off by a particular decodable series, I encourage you to seek out others.

Lastly, it's important to remember that decodable texts should not be the only texts students experience. Be sure to give them plenty of encounters with rich, authentic texts. The value of reading aloud to students as

"It is late," said Kate. "I need to take Dave his cake."

Kate saw Dave's pal Wade at a lake. Wave, wave!

well as scaffolding them into complex text is unmistakable and helps build vocabulary and background knowledge.

They are babyish!

Not all decodable texts are designed for kindergartners. While many are designed for young children who are just starting out on their reading journey, there are several geared to older readers that provide practice opportunities for more advanced phonics skills.

Also, don't underestimate the power of basic decodables for older students who are learning to read, including those who are learning to read English as another language. They generate a safe place for practice while providing opportunities for confirmation and success.

"The types of words which appear in beginning reading texts may well exert a more powerful influence in shaping word identification strategies than the method of reading instruction (Juel & Roper/Schneider, 1985)." If you teach beginning readers, I can't emphasize enough the benefits of using decodable texts. They are the best tools for teaching beginner readers to decode! They allow students to apply the phonics skills you've been teaching them and, therefore, develop automatic, accurate word reading. Best of all, these decodable books will help them build confidence and feel success. Replace predictable, repetitive texts with decodable ones.

What to Look for in a Decodable Book Series

- The series follows a logical scope and sequence that progresses from simple to complex phonics skills. Consider how the sequence of skills aligns to your phonics program.
- Each book has plenty of words that follow the target skill.
- Each book has a limited number of irregular words.
- Each book's language and storyline make sense.

Transition Out of Decodables

Decodable texts are like training wheels: Kids need them for only a short amount of time. The goal is to transition away from them as soon as the child is ready. They are just a stepping stone. Once students have a strong phonics base and no guessing habit, move them into authentic texts (i.e., trade books).

The percentage of decodable words in books should vary so that you can gradually transition your students to trade books. Some books are highly decodable, containing at least 90 percent of words with sound-spelling correspondences that the students have learned. Other books are less decodable, containing closer to 75–80 percent. Having a range enables me to move students gradually from books with a higher decodability percentage to books with a lower decodability percentage and then to authentic texts. It ensures a smooth transition and gives me confidence that each student is ready to attack more difficult texts, without having to rely on cueing strategies. If I notice a student struggling with an authentic text, making numerous errors and resorting to guessing, I know he needs more practice with and support in decodable texts, as well as more scaffolding in transitioning to the authentic text.

Knowing when a student is ready to move out of decodables is not an exact science. Farrell and Hunter provide their preferred guidelines for moving students away from decodable texts and into authentic texts (2021). Students should be able to:

1. Accurately read real and nonsense CVC, CCVC, and CVCC words (short vowels, digraphs, consonant clusters) in isolation.

2. Decode two-syllable real words (e.g., *comment*, *napkin*) and familiar three-syllable words (e.g., *penmanship*, *fantastic*) in isolation that contain short-vowel syllables (closed) or schwa.

3. Decode one- and two-syllable real words with *r*-controlled vowels (e.g., *bird*, *party*) and silent *e* (e.g., *hope*, *reptile*).

Instructional Implications

Decodable texts have enormous implications for small-group and whole-group instruction.

Small-Group Instruction

My favorite part of the day is working with my students in small groups, using decodable texts. It's so satisfying giving them time to practice applying skills and providing them with immediate feedback. Small-group time is valuable to me, too, because it enables me to get to know my students as readers.

Watch a small-group lesson using a decodable text.

Instead of organizing your students by guided reading levels, I suggest organizing them by phonics skills and giving them decodable texts that align with those skills. If students make an excessive number of mistakes during their reading of the text, that text is too difficult, and you can select a less demanding one. Additionally, if you have students whose reading skills are advanced enough that they don't require decodable texts, give them authentic texts, or trade books, to read.

Consider following these steps for small-group instruction.

Before Reading

After teaching an explicit whole-class lesson on the phonics skill you plan to focus on (e.g., *oa* words), quickly review it at the start of small-group time. Then have students read words that contain the target skill (e.g., *boat*, *toad*, *soak*). I write and display the words on my small, tabletop dry-erase board. Another option is to have students look for target words in the text itself. Also, teach or review the high-frequency words that appear in the text.

Download blank template for a small-group decodable text routine.

Small-Group Decodable Text Routine

Before Reading
- Review target skill.
- Read and write words that contain the target skill.
- Pre-teach or review any irregular high-frequency words.

During Reading
- Have students read the text, while providing feedback and support.

After Reading
- Ask questions about the text.

During Reading

This is where I spend the majority of our small-group time. I have all students read aloud the text at the same time, but at different points in the book to ensure that no one just echoes what a classmate says, and is actually decoding the words. It might sound chaotic, but it's not! Model the low volume level that you would like students to use. Then give a book to every other student at the table. For example, if there are five students at the table, give a book to the students in spots 1, 3, and 5.

Ask those three students to start reading their books aloud, at the volume level you modeled. Have students 2 and 4 continue to read the target-skill word list. Once students 1, 3, and 5 finish the first page or paragraph, hand books to students 2 and 4 to begin reading. As students read aloud, lean in and listen closely to each one and provide any necessary feedback. Guide them to develop a habit of accurate reading. As students finish the book,

direct them to start reading it again and continue until you tell them to stop. This process maximizes the amount of time each student spends reading.

After Reading

Ask comprehension questions to monitor students' understanding of the text. It's okay to save the deep discussions for later, when you are reading grade-level texts or during read-alouds. Decodable texts usually lack the complexity of grade-level texts, so your questions are likely to be more literal in nature. We know there are better materials to develop language comprehension than decodables.

Be sure to review the "Strategies for Success" in Moves 3 and 6 for more tips in working with students in small groups.

Whole-Group Instruction

Give students plenty of opportunities to practice the phonics skills you are teaching in your whole-group lessons. Specifically, give them opportunities to transfer isolated skills to connected text. This allows them meaningful practice decoding words that contain the targeted skill. While some students may only need a few practice opportunities to develop automaticity, others will need many more. Here is the procedure I used with my second graders:

1. Display two or three decodable sentences with words that contain the target skill.

2. Point to the first sentence and give students a minute to read it silently.

3. Have students choral-read the sentence. Listen carefully to ensure they're reading accurately and provide assistance as needed.

4. Ask a literal comprehension question about the sentence to ensure students are attending to its meaning and focusing on the text. For example, if they read the sentence, "Troy left the shop to avoid the noise," you could ask, "Why did Troy leave the shop?"

5. Repeat the process for the remaining sentences.

Generally, I don't spend as much time using decodable texts in whole-group instruction because I find them more valuable in small-group instruction, where I can provide differentiation and immediate, targeted feedback. Choral reading can be problematic because some students will simply parrot what they hear their classmates say, rather than decoding words themselves. One way to combat that is by giving each student a copy of the text and asking them to track the words with a finger as the class reads it together. With my move to first grade, I have started doing the following activity:

Watch the Text Transfer procedure.

1. Give each student a copy of the decodable text.

2. Give them 1–2 minutes to highlight the target-skill words in the text. If they finish before the time is up, have them whisper-read the highlighted words.

3. Have students read the highlighted words as a class, individually, or with a partner.

4. Choral-read the entire passage together as a class or have students partner-read it with a classmate.

5. Ask questions about the passage or have students retell it to a partner.

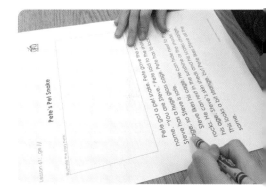

These transfer processes allow many exposures to words that contain your chosen target skill. Adapt them as necessary to work for your population of students.

Whole-Group Decodable Text Routine

Before Reading

- Give students 1–2 minutes to highlight target-skill words in the text.
- Have students read highlighted words as a class, with a partner, or independently.

During Reading

- Invite students to choral-read the text as a class or with partners.

After Reading

- Have student retell the story and answer questions about the text.

Download blank template for a whole-group decodable text routine.

Strategies for Success

Here are some practical strategies for using decodable texts in your classroom.

Commit, Repurpose, and Reorganize

Commit to giving your brand-new readers decodable texts to practice decoding. This does not mean you have to get rid of all your leveled texts. Since leveled texts are simply books that can be categorized into different levels of difficulty, they can include predictable, repetitive texts as well as authentic trade books. Of course we do not want to get rid of all our books! Consider repurposing predictable texts for instruction that builds oral language, vocabulary, writing skills, and creativity (Goldberg, 2021). Reorganize your books by topic instead of level for students to peruse in their free time. We want students to be excited about books, so never limit books for them to explore on their own. Expand their choices! You will need these authentic texts available for when students are ready to read them.

Start Your Decodable Book Collection

Your goal should be to have decodable books that match your phonics scope and sequence. If books were created specifically for your program, make acquiring them a priority. Additionally, collect a variety of decodable books from different publishers and align them with your program. Review the books for high-frequency words and how they are used (more on that in Move 5). A few of them are okay, but not the majority. Most of the words should be decodable.

Building your decodable library will take time and resources. The first thing I suggest is to search your school for available books. Check unoccupied classrooms or that odd cupboard in the workroom, and you may just find an older set of decodables to use.

I got the majority of my decodable books by writing DonorsChoose grants. Check it out: donorschoose.org. It's a great resource to get what you need.

Don't be afraid to ask your administrator for help. Last year, I had my eye on rich decodable texts designed to build students' knowledge. But they were offered only as one large, expensive set. I knew it was a long shot, but I decided to take a chance and ask my principal for the funds to purchase it, armed with some information about the benefits of the texts. I was overjoyed when she agreed to purchase the entire set! Slowly but surely my collection has grown over the years.

Take a Multiple-Text Approach

Having students read decodable books is a wonderful way to help them practice phonics skills you are teaching. But those books should not be the only books students are exposed to. Our students can read to learn at the same time they are learning to read. So even though you are giving them decodables to read, you should also be providing rich read-alouds and scaffolding them into more complex text to build their knowledge. According to Cervetti and Hiebert, "Even while students are learning to read words, they can and should have opportunities to build knowledge from texts with worthwhile ideas and words" (2018).

By using a variety of texts, you help students develop all necessary reading skills. Decodable texts give them practice in transferring phonics skills to connected text. Grade-level and read-aloud texts expose them to more advanced concepts, genres, and vocabulary, and build background knowledge. They enable you to lead rich discussions and strengthen oral language skills.

With my first and second graders, I use decodable sentences and/or passages in whole-group phonics lessons. For whole-group vocabulary and comprehension lessons, I use authentic grade-level texts so students grapple with more complex material. During small-group time, I use a variety of text types, depending on the needs of students in the groups. I end the day with an engaging read-aloud that raises the roof on students' listening comprehension. Decodable texts are definitely not the *only* type of text my students experience.

> **Types of Texts to Use**
>
> **Decodable Texts:** Students apply their phonics skills to connected text.
>
> **Authentic Grade-Level Texts:** Students read complex text, with teacher support and scaffolding.
>
> **Read-Aloud Texts:** Teachers read books that students are not able to read themselves.

Use Whisper Tubes

Using whisper tubes is another way to encourage all students to decode. There are many variations of these, from the do-it-yourself PVC pipe variety to commercially created ones. Students love being able to speak into the tube—or "phone" as it's sometimes called—and hear themselves as they read. The tube amplifies their voice, which can be helpful to students who struggle to hear and process the sounds in spoken language (phonological awareness).

Give Immediate Feedback

Be positive with students and point out what they do well. When they struggle to decode a word, tell them the sound they missed and have them blend all the sounds. For example, if a student reads "main" as "man," point to the *ai* and say, "These two letters spell /ay/. What sound?" Then have them blend the three sounds: /m/ /ay/ /n/. In other words, don't just tell them the word. Let them work through and decode it themselves, with assistance from you as necessary. This is your time to coach students as they sit in the driver's seat. And remember, do not encourage students to use pictures to figure out the word. However, *do* encourage them to look at pictures after they've read the page to enhance the meaning and understand the full context of the story.

Encourage Students to Be Word Detectives

Being a "word detective" is a fun way to encourage students to focus on a phonics skill you are teaching. As they are reading the decodable text, every time they come to a word that contains the target skill, ask them to make a noise (e.g., click their tongue, tap the table, snap fingers, etc.). For example, let's say you taught the grapheme *ee*. As students are reading their book in small group, you might have them snap their fingers every time they read a word that contains *ee* (e.g., *seed, teeth, eel*).

Create a Take-Home Book System

Consider setting up a system for students to check out decodable texts from your classroom so they can practice applying their learning at home. My first graders take home three decodable books on Mondays and return them on Fridays. I encourage them to read each book at least three times to a parent or caregiver to strengthen their decoding skills. They are so excited to show off what they can do to adults at home. I make sure to provide reading tips for family members, so they know how to best support their beginning reader.

Watch a video for parents and caregivers with tips for reading with children.

To supplement my decodable book collection, I purchased a set of downloadable books, printed them out and laminated them, and bound them into mini-books. That way, if they get lost, it isn't costly for me to replace them.

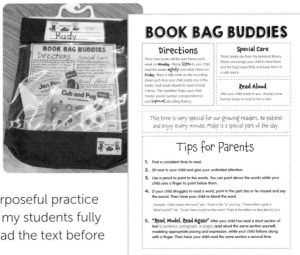

Decodable books provide the targeted, purposeful practice my students need. It's so rewarding to see my students fully engaged, confident, and on task as they read the text before them. That's the power of decodables!

In Closing, Remember...

- Beginning readers typically "read" predictable, repetitive texts by memorizing the pattern or guessing words from the context and pictures.
- Predictable, repetitive texts create an illusion of reading and, unless you look closely, the student's inability to read is hidden from view.
- Decodable texts are a tool that allows targeted, purposeful practice of the phonics skills you are teaching.
- Decodable texts are only decodable if you have taught the phonics skills featured in them.
- Align your decodable book collection to your phonics scope and sequence.
- Decodables should be used for a limited period of time, similar to training wheels. You should transition students out of them as soon as they are ready.
- Decodable texts should never be the only type of book students experience. You should support students in grade-level texts and read aloud more complex authentic texts to them.
- The more you understand about phonics concepts, the better you'll understand decodable texts.

KEEP Giving students opportunities to read books.

STOP Giving beginning readers predictable texts to learn how to read.

START Using decodable texts with beginning readers.

Embrace a Better Approach to Teaching "Sight Words"

When I visited a kindergarten classroom during the first week of school one year, the teacher was working on the word *from* with the kids. After quite a bit of instruction, she excitedly asked them, "So what's our sight word of the day?" The bewildered students simply stared at her, until one of them perked up and shouted, "F!" Most kindergartners are still learning the difference between a letter and word, and yet many programs insist on teaching them a high number of high-frequency words. I am disheartened when I see the pressures some districts place on young children (and their teachers!), demanding they memorize 50, 75, even over 100 such words.

In my early days of teaching, I thought "sight words" were words that could not be sounded out. So, I taught them as whole units to be memorized visually. I have since learned that teaching those words that way inhibits how the brain learns and stores them (Miles & Ehri, 2019; Yoncheva et al., 2015). For words to be instantly retrieved when they are seen in print, their graphemes, phonemes, and meanings need to be linked in long-term memory. It's critical that students match a word's individual sounds with its graphemes. When we focus on the entire word, with the goal of memorizing it, we limit the process necessary for storing those words. Students *need* to sound out the word, even when its spelling is not phonetically regular.

> Many people believe we must memorize words as whole units because the English language is largely irregular and inconsistent. However, it is more regular and consistent than you might think.

Many people believe we must memorize words as whole units because the English language is largely irregular and inconsistent. However, it is more regular and consistent than you might think. About 50 percent of all English words can be spelled accurately by sound-symbol rules alone, and another 36 percent can be spelled accurately except for one speech sound (Hanna et al., 1966). Even more words could be considered regular and consistent if their meaning and origin are taken into account. Moats (2020) suggests that only four percent of all the words in print today are truly irregular.

One of the biggest problems with memorizing words as units is that the number of words a student can memorize is limited. Diane McGuinness (1999) found that most people can remember only about 1,500 to 2,000 abstract visual symbols. In other words, a whole-word writing system simply cannot work. Sure, students may be able to memorize words initially, but eventually they will reach their memory threshold and begin to flounder. Additionally, Yoncheva et al. (2015) found that beginning readers who focus on letter-sound relationships, instead of memorizing whole words, increase activity in the area of the brain best wired for reading. So *how* we teach words and what we draw students' attention to (or what we don't) have a wide-ranging and lasting impact.

Furthermore, if students lean too heavily on memorizing words as whole units, they will be more likely to confuse similar-looking words. When my son with dyslexia was in kindergarten, memorizing "sight words" was a huge focus and something we practiced a lot. Years later, he would continue to mix up words such as "said" and "and," and "from" and "for." These are words that he memorized as whole units, and if you look at them, they are visually similar. He had never closely analyzed the letters and sounds within the words.

You may also notice repercussions when students attempt to spell memorized words. You may see a word that is phonetically regular, but the student still spells it incorrectly. For example, she may spell the word *went* like this: *wnet*. One explanation for this is that students memorize a random string of letters instead of mapping the letters and sounds. If you see students making errors such as these, there is a good chance they are attempting to memorize words as whole units.

When students become such expert memorizers, their limited ability to decode goes undercover. They may use their ability to memorize words and guess from context to hide the fact that they lack solid phoneme-grapheme knowledge. And the longer we wait to intervene, the deeper the hole becomes for them to climb out of. As they move up the grade levels, it becomes less likely they will have a teacher who is knowledgeable about beginning reading skills. We then tend to get students in middle school and high school receiving a fluency or comprehension intervention, when what they really need is basic phonics and decoding intervention. It requires a close look to catch these students before they fall through the cracks.

One way I can determine if this is an issue for my young students is by looking at our universal screening data. I use Acadience Reading (formerly known as DIBELS Next), which is designed for universal screening and progress monitoring. The data I get from this assessment is invaluable to me. When I see a student whose words-correct-per-minute score is okay, but his nonsense-word fluency score isn't, it is a good indication that he may have a memorizing and guessing problem. A student's ability to decode nonsense words, or lack thereof, provides a window into his knowledge of letter-sound correspondences and ability to blend sounds.

Because of the general assumption that "sight words" cannot be sounded out and must be memorized, popular approaches to teaching them include drills, flash cards, worksheets, and the tedious task of writing them over and over. Additionally, many educators believe that students can learn words by their visual shapes. They outline the shape of a word to reinforce its visual form to help students memorize how it looks. However, Ehri (2004) states that words are not read by their shape, contextual guessing, or whole-word memorization.

What if there was a more effective way?

"Sight Words" Explained

In this section, I clear up the term "sight word," along with terms related to it.

Let's Clear Up the Term "Sight Word"

Most teachers use the term "sight word" to describe a word that appears frequently in text. They generally think of these words as whole units that can't be decoded and, therefore, must be memorized as whole units. We need to dispel that idea. In contrast, reading researchers and literacy experts use the term "sight word" in a much different way. Take, for example, what Linnea Ehri says, "Words that have become sight words are read from memory. Sight of the word immediately activates both pronunciation and meaning. To build sight words, orthographic mapping is required. Readers must form connections between spellings and pronunciations of specific words by applying knowledge

Terms to Know

High-Frequency Word: A word that occurs often in text.

Orthographic Mapping: A process that involves connecting pronunciations of phonemes in a word to the graphemes that represent those pronunciations and linking them to the word's meaning to store the word in long-term memory

Sight Word: Any word that can be retrieved from memory instantly because it has been orthographically mapped

Regular High-Frequency Word: A word that occurs often in text and has consistent, reliable sound-spelling correspondences (e.g., *can*, *that*)

Temporarily Irregular High-Frequency Word: A word that occurs often in text and is decodable once students have learned the phonics skills it contains (e.g., *like*, *for*)

Permanently Irregular High-Frequency Word: A word that occurs frequently in text and has irregular sound-spelling correspondences (e.g., *said*, *one*)

of the general writing system. When readers see a new word, and say or hear its pronunciation, its spelling becomes mapped onto its pronunciation and meaning. It's the connections that serve to 'glue' spelling to pronunciations in memory" (2014).

David Kilpatrick (2015), explains sight words, "A *sight word* is a word that is instantly and effortlessly recalled from memory, regardless of whether it is phonically regular or irregular. A *sight-word vocabulary* refers to the pool of words a student can effortlessly recognize."

In other words, any word that can be recognized automatically is a sight word. That does not mean the reader has memorized the word as a whole unit, but that she has mapped its spelling and pronunciation and, in so doing, is able to retrieve it instantly. Sight-word reading is the end goal. We want all words to become sight words for students because it is the most efficient way to read words (Miles & Ehri, 2019).

"Every word wants to be a sight word when it grows up."

—Jan Wasowicz

My son and I read together every night. He reads aloud to me, and I assist and model as necessary. Each word he reads automatically and effortlessly has become a sight word for him. Any word that he needs to sound out has not. I remember him carefully but accurately decoding the word *un-cer-e-mo-ni-ous-ly*. Although I admired his attention to each letter and letter cluster in the word, he had not committed the spelling of the word to memory for instant recall...yet. With more opportunities to decode the word, it would have become stored in his long-term memory and could then have been considered a sight word, or a word he recognized automatically.

Instead of "sight words," a more appropriate term for words we see often in print is "high-frequency words." So I suggest using "sight word" as reading researchers do when they describe *any* word that students can recognize instantly and effortlessly. Again, that does not mean they have memorized the word as a whole unit, but that they have analyzed the grapheme-phoneme correspondences and connected them to the word's meaning. This enables the orthographic mapping process to take place and the word can then be retrieved from memory immediately.

Let's Clear Up the Term "Orthographic Mapping"

As discussed in Move 3, orthographic mapping is the process we use to store words into long-term memory (Ehri, 2014). For that to happen, students must link a word's spelling (orthography), the pronunciation (phonology), and the meaning (semantics). Orthographic mapping is not based on visual memorization of words but on connections the reader makes between written letters and pronunciations that represent those letters (Miles & Ehri, 2019). Phonemic awareness and knowledge of letter sounds are central to the orthographic mapping process. Since this process is something that occurs in the brain, it is not something we can actually see or teach, but it is something we help to *facilitate* by providing students with opportunities for orthographic mapping to occur. This may seem like a small difference, but it's important to understand.

Let's Clear Up the Terms "Phonetically Regular" and "Phonetically Irregular"

Two other terms that are important to recognize when it comes to high-frequency words are phonetically regular and phonetically irregular.

Phonetically regular words have sound-spelling relationships that are consistent and reliable. For example, consider the word *that*. Once you've taught students that *th* represents the voiced sound /th/, the short /ă/ sound, and the consonant-*t* sound, *that* is completely regular and decodable.

Phonetically irregular words contain sounds or spellings that are not consistent and reliable. For example, the word *said* is considered irregular because *ai* is an infrequent spelling for the short /ě/ sound. Because "phonetically irregular words" is a mouthful for students, I call them "heart words," but I have heard many other great options such as irregular words, snap words, flash words, tricky words, sticky words, red words, exceptions, and rule-breakers. Whatever term you use, instead of focusing your efforts on getting students to memorize the words, intensify your focus on the phonemes and the graphemes that represent them.

Let's Clear Up the Terms "Temporarily Irregular" and "Permanently Irregular"

Phonetically irregular words can be organized into two categories: temporarily irregular and permanently irregular. How you decide which category a word belongs in depends on your students' phoneme-grapheme knowledge and the concepts you plan to teach in your phonics lessons. For example, *his* is an irregular word for students until they are taught that the letter *s* can represent the /z/ phoneme, as well as the /s/ phoneme.

Keep in mind, there are degrees of regularity within words. We need to be mindful of the words *and* of the learner. For kindergarteners, the word *see* is most likely irregular and their teacher will need to draw their attention to the *ee* spelling. However, for first or second graders who have learned that *ee* represents the long /ē/ sound, *see* has a very reliable spelling and would no longer be considered an irregular word. Another example is the word *young*. While phonetically regular, the short /ŭ/ sound is not the most common sound for the *ou* grapheme. So, it's helpful to consider irregular and regular on a continuum.

In contrast, the word *people* is permanently irregular because *eo* is always an unusual spelling for the long /ē/ sound, so it will need extra attention and practice.

See the table to the left (Miles et al., 2017) for an example of how the first set of words from the Dolch word list might be categorized by phonetically regular, temporarily irregular, or permanently irregular.

First Dolch Word List		
Regularly Spelled	**Temporarily Irregularly Spelled**	**Permanently Irregularly Spelled**
and	away	a
big	blue	come
can	down	one
go	find	said
help	for	the
I	funny	to
in	here	two
is	little	where
it	look	
jump	make	
me	my	
not	play	
red	see	
run	three	
up	yellow	
we	you	

Instructional Implications

Sight-word learning doesn't happen by sight. As recommended in Move 3, let orthographic mapping guide you as you think about your instruction. If we teach students to connect the phonemes and graphemes in a word, rather than memorize them as a whole unit, the number of words they can learn is endless. Research from Yoncheva et al. (2015) shows increased brain activity among beginning readers who focus on letter-sound relationships, instead of whole words, in the area of their brains best wired for reading. Students need to notice those sound-spelling connections, even when they are irregular, for orthographic mapping to occur. We can set students up for success in reading by giving them a strong foundation in phonemic awareness and phonics, as well as adding in some instruction for irregular high-frequency words.

Even permanently irregular words have some consistent spellings within them, which can serve as anchors to support decoding. Consider the word *said*. The first and final phonemes /s/ and /d/ are represented by the very regular spellings of *s* and *d*. Students can use these sounds as anchors that will help them as they sound out the word. There is just one violator that we can draw students' attention to: *ai* as an irregular spelling for the sound /ĕ/. If a student forgets the unusual sound-spelling, often the consistent spellings can help them remember the inconsistent ones. For example, when reading the word *what*, one of my students would initially say the short-*a* sound, "/w/ /ă/ /t/." Then he would correct himself by changing the vowel sound and correctly pronouncing the word *what*.

Encourage students to analyze the word all the way through so they anchor regular spellings and sounds, and draw their attention to the irregular spellings and sounds. Then give them opportunities to sound out and write the words, and analyze the internal units, so orthographic mapping can take place. In other words, give them plenty of chances to interact with the phoneme-grapheme relationships in the word.

Strategies for Success

Here are some strategies for teaching high-frequency words in your classroom:

Organize Your High-Frequency Word List

Separate your high-frequency word list into regular and irregular spellings to determine which words you will need to teach as "heart words." Then integrate the regular high-frequency words in your phonics lessons. Doing that will reduce the number of words you need to teach separately.

From there, compare your list of words to your phonics scope and sequence to determine which words are temporarily irregular and permanently irregular. As you do that, remember that students' knowledge is imperative, and the regularity of a word's spelling exists on a continuum. The more you understand about phonics, the English language, and your scope and sequence, the easier it will be to sort words productively.

Group Your Words

Based on your phonics scope and sequence, decide on the best time to teach irregular words (whether temporary or permanent). Group words with similar patterns together. For example, you could teach *go, no, so, he, be,* and *she* together when you introduce open syllables. Also consider words that you may need to teach sooner than later. For example, if your decodable books include the word *the*, you will need to teach that word well before you come to the digraph-*th* lesson in your phonics scope and sequence.

Teach Irregular Words Using an Explicit Routine

How to Teach Irregular Words

1. Say the word and use it in a sentence.
2. Segment and count the sounds.
3. Map the phonemes (sounds) to the graphemes (spellings).
4. Point out the irregular parts.
5. Cover the word and have students rewrite it from memory.
6. Uncover the word and check students' spelling.
7. Have students generate sentences that contain the word.

Download steps in teaching irregular words.

Here is the step-by-step protocol I use for teaching irregular words explicitly, based on the work of Nora Chahbazi and the EBLI (*Evidence-Based Literacy Instruction*) program (see more here: https://eblireads.com/ebli-webinars/). You can use tokens and the printouts of the sound boxes or individual dry-erase boards and markers.

Watch how I teach my whole class irregular words.

Download blank Elkonin Box template.

1. **Say the word and use it in a sentence to give it meaning and context.**

   Repeating the word in context shows students the function of the word.

   "The heart word we will learn today is *said*. What word? (said). Her mom *said* it was time to clean her room."

2. **Segment and count the sounds.**

   Introduce the word verbally before writing it or showing a spelled-out form of it. David Kilpatrick (2016) explains that when students can concentrate on the oral properties of the word, they will be in a better position to map the phonemes of the word to the graphemes. Have students orally segment the word and count the number of sounds.

   "Tell me the sounds you hear in the word *said*. (/s/ /ĕ/ /d/). How many sounds? (3). That's right."

   Have students orally segment the word again, but this time have them push tokens up in the cells of an Elkonin Box, or create lines on their whiteboard for each sound.

3. **Map the phonemes (sounds) to the graphemes (spellings).**

   Show students the word and help them connect each spelling within it to the sound it represents.

"What's the first sound? (/s/) Yes. Say /s/ as you write *s* in the first box." You will write an *s* in the first box (or on the first line if you are using individual dry-erase boards) and the students will too.

Then ask, "What's the next sound? (/ĕ/) What letter usually spells the /ĕ/ sound? *E*. But in this word, /ĕ/ is spelled with the letters *ai*." Write *ai* and then have students follow. Encourage them to say the /ĕ/ sound while they write the unusual spelling.

Finally ask, "What's the last sound? (/d/) Say /d/ as you write the *d*."

4. **Point out the irregular parts.**

Next, help the "tricky" to become "sticky." Now that you have helped students connect the phonemes and graphemes, draw their attention to the irregular or "tricky" part of the word. You might have students draw a heart either above or around it.

Or have them highlight it.

Another option is to simply have them circle it, which is what I do because many students find it difficult to draw a heart.

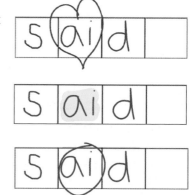

Ask students how many letters spell the /ĕ/ sound and then have them draw that number of lines under that part. You might say, "Two letters spell the /ĕ/ sound, so let's put two lines under the *ai* spelling." This is another way to draw students' attention to the tricky parts of words.

5. **Cover the word and have students rewrite it from memory.**

   Cover the word. Then have students erase it and rewrite it from memory. You may want to have students erase the letters, but leave the lines and circles as a reminder of where the tricky part goes.

   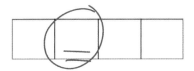 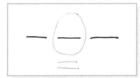

   Ask students to fill in the word from memory, using the lines and circle(s) to help them remember the spellings.

    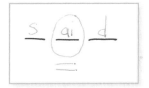

6. **Uncover the word and check students' spelling.**

   Show students the word and have them check and, if necessary, correct their spellings. Last, have students erase everything and rewrite the word, without lines or circles.

7. **Have students generate sentences that contain the word.**

   Generating sentences that contain the word helps students to understand its meaning and function (Miles & Ehri, 2017). Many irregular high-frequency words are function words, such as *of*, *for*, and *is*, which can be especially difficult to learn. So it's helpful for students to contextualize them to reinforce what they mean and how to use them, especially for students who are learning the English language (Miles & Ehri, 2017). After students have come up with a sentence, have them turn to a classmate and say it, and then have some partners share their sentences with the whole group. Another option, depending on the grade level of your students, is to have them write their sentences on a dry-erase board or paper, and then read them to one another.

Provide Lots of Opportunities to Practice

Remember, some students will need more practice opportunities than other students do. Provide students with lots of opportunities to spell and read high-frequency words. Repeat the protocol for teaching irregular words described earlier in your small-group instruction, as necessary. After explicitly teaching the words, review them using flash cards and encouraging students to analyze the internal units of each word to decode it. Consider surrounding the irregular part of the word with a circle or heart to call attention to it. You can also have students practice reading words in phrases, sentences, decodable books, and authentic texts, such as trade books.

Use a Sound-Spelling Wall

Consider using a sound-spelling wall to help students map words' spellings and sounds. You can refer students to the wall as you review the various graphemes for each sound. See page 30 for a detailed discussion.

Analyze the Phoneme-Grapheme Connections

Review the word by asking students detailed questions to help them analyze phoneme-grapheme connections. For example, show students the word *was* and ask, "What letter spells the sound /w/? (*w*) What letter spells the sound /z/? (*s*) What letter spells the sound /ŭ/? (*a*)." You could also flip these questions to help students analyze grapheme-phoneme connections. For example, "In the word *was*, what sound does the letter *a* spell? (/ŭ/). What sound does the *s* spell? (/z/)."

Watch an analysis of phonemes and graphemes.

Sound Out Words... Literally!

Do you sometimes sound out words exactly as they're spelled, instead of how they're pronounced, to remember the spelling? For example, when I spell the word *Wednesday*, I say to myself, "Wed-nes-day." My students love to do something similar. I vividly remember teaching my second graders the word *friend*, using the protocol for teaching irregular words on page 102. After learning that the /ĕ/ sound in *friend* is spelled with the letters *i* and *e*, they started to pronounce the word as "fry-end" every time they wrote it. It was a silly trick that got them laughing and writing, while also helping them remember how to spell the words.

Tell Students Word Parts When Necessary

When students struggle to recognize an irregular word as they're reading, give them the irregular sound and have them reblend it. For example, if a student comes to the word *weight* and stops, point to the *w* and have her say the sound /w/. Then point to the *eigh* and tell her the sound /ay/. Point to the *t* and have her say the sound /t/. Lastly, encourage her to blend the sounds and say *weight*.

Spin, Say, Write

My students love to play "Spin, Say, Write" to practice irregular words. I start by writing six words on a pie chart template and then make photocopies. With a partner, students take turns spinning a paper clip, using the pencil tip to anchor it on the pie chart, and seeing where it lands. They read the word that the paper clip lands on and then write the word while saying its sounds. It's a great way to review irregular high-frequency words, especially before we read a text that contains them.

Download blank template for Spin, Say, Write.

In Closing, Remember...

- Memorizing words as a whole unit inhibits the process that is necessary to store words in long-term memory.
- Instead of focusing our efforts on getting students to memorize words, we need to intensify our focus on phonemes and the graphemes that represent them.
- Every word wants to be a sight word when it grows up! Making sure words become part of a student's sight-word vocabulary is the goal.
- The process necessary for words to become sight words is called orthographic mapping.
- Orthographic mapping involves the student linking a word's spelling, pronunciation, and meaning.
- High-frequency words can be regular and irregular.
- Irregular high-frequency words can be further categorized by "temporarily irregular" and "permanently irregular." Permanently irregular words will require extra attention and practice.
- We must consider students' phonics knowledge as we choose words to teach.
- Use an explicit protocol to teach high-frequency words—one that assists students in mapping the word's internal sounds to their spellings.
- Draw students' attention to the word's regular parts and irregular parts.
- Students may need several exposures to a word before they are able to map it.

KEEP Teaching students irregular high-frequency words.

STOP Requiring students to memorize large lists of words as whole units, especially those with consistent reliable spellings (e.g., *that*, *can*).

START Encouraging students to map words' sounds (phonemes) with their graphemes (spellings), whether the words are regular or irregular.

Focus on Meaningful Fluency Practice

One time I heard a teacher ask, "Why does it matter if he reads slowly as long as he got most of the words right?" While speed-reading should not be our goal, we *do* want our students to be able to read at a reasonable rate because it has a direct impact on their comprehension. When students spend so much of their cognitive energy in decoding, they cannot read efficiently and thoughtfully, and their comprehension suffers. They are focusing so intensely on retrieving sound-symbol correspondences from memory that there is little room left to think about what they are reading. On the other hand, when students retrieve sound-symbol correspondences automatically, they can focus on meaning (Ardoin et al., 2013). Decoding becomes effortless, which frees up students' working memory so they can think more deeply about the text.

"Developing students' fluent reading is perhaps one of the most complex and comprehensive tasks teachers undertake."

—Melissa Orkin et al.

Fluency is sometimes defined as simply "reading fast," and it's easy to see why, considering we often measure it by timing students' oral reading. But there is so much more to reading fluency! It's not all about how quickly we read.

Fluency Explained

The National Reading Panel (2000) defines fluency as "the ability to recognize words easily, read with greater speed, accuracy and expression, and to better understand what is read." When students are fluent, they recognize words automatically and are able to read for meaning. Reading comprehension is the goal, and fluency provides a bridge between word recognition and comprehension (Duke & Cartwright, 2021).

Many underlying skills contribute to reading fluency. Often, fluency goals are set for students who lack the foundational skills necessary to read fluently. Those students may need more explicit instruction in phonemic awareness and/or phonics, or more meaningful opportunities to practice and internalize sound-symbol correspondences. When we address the foundational skills of reading, fluency evolves from there (Ecalle et al., 2021). So before setting fluency goals, consider your students' phonemic awareness, letter-sound knowledge, and decoding skills. "The best candidates for fluency interventions are students with slow, accurate reading." (Hudson et al., 2022)

Fluency is most often described as a combination of accuracy, rate, and prosody. While it is more complex than integrating those three skills, they remain its cornerstones (Hasbrouck, 2020). Let's explore the meaning of each one.

Accuracy

Accuracy means reading the words correctly, and should be, as Hasbrouck and Glaser put it, "First, foremost, and forever the foundation of fluency (2019)." We want students to read a high number of words in a text accurately. To do that, they need a strong foundation in phonics and lots of opportunities to apply phonics skills. That means we should be attending to decoding accuracy from the time children begin learning to read. When students misread many words, don't push them to read faster. That will not benefit them and, in fact, could delay growth in fluent word-identification skills (Torgesen, 2020). Instead, determine the underlying, foundational skills they need and teach them accordingly. A reasonable target for accuracy is 98 percent (Parker & Burns, 2014), which is high enough to maintain comprehension of most texts. An initial goal for a child who is misreading a high number of words might be for him to slow down to ensure he is attending to accuracy.

Rate

Rate refers to the speed at which students read words. To develop an adequate reading rate, students need automaticity, which is the ability to recognize letters, letter patterns, and words automatically. Those subskills must be effortless so students can devote their attention to the text's meaning.

You can calculate rate by dividing the number of words a student reads correctly by the total amount of time in minutes that it took the student to read them (words correct per minute; WCPM). For example, after a student reads a passage for three minutes, count the number of words she read correctly (e.g., 144) and divide it by the number of minutes (e.g., 3) to get her WCPM score (e.g., 48). Self-corrections the student makes within two seconds should not be counted as errors, but any word the student misreads or skips should be. Another approach that combines accuracy and rate, and yields an accuracy percentage, is to time the student for just one minute on a grade-level passage and calculate the total number of words he reads correctly. For example, after a student reads a passage for one minute, count the number of words he read correctly (e.g., 82) and you have his WCPM score of 82. Divide the number of words read correctly (e.g., 82) by the total words he read (e.g., 90) to get his accuracy percentage (e.g., 91%). This is a reliable way to get a general sense of students' overall reading ability. Because timing each student for just one minute sets the same standard for all students, you can determine which students are becoming proficient and which aren't. You'll be surprised by how much information you can glean in just one minute. Think of this assessment as a thermometer to measure if a student is on track or needs more support. According to Hasbrouck, "Calculating WCPM serves as an accurate and powerful indicator of overall reading competence— especially through its strong correlation with comprehension" (2006).

Once you have a student's WCPM score, compare it to fluency norms to see if she is on target. Hasbrouck and Tindal updated their fluency norms in 2017 (see below). They compiled the norms using three popular assessments: DIBELS, DIBELS Next/Acadience, and easy CBM. If a student scores at the 50th percentile or above, he is at the target, appropriate rate. If a student scores below the 50th percentile, he is likely experiencing some difficulty in reading.

Oral Reading Fluency Norms

Grade	Percentile	Fall WCPM*	Winter WCPM*	Spring WCPM*
1	90		97	116
	75		59	91
	50		29	60
	25		16	34
	10		9	18
2	90	111	131	148
	75	84	109	124
	50	50	84	100
	25	36	59	72
	10	23	35	43
3	90	134	161	166
	75	104	137	139
	50	83	97	112
	25	59	79	91
	10	40	62	63

Grade	Percentile	Fall WCPM*	Winter WCPM*	Spring WCPM*
4	90	153	168	184
	75	125	143	160
	50	94	120	133
	25	75	95	105
	10	60	71	83
5	90	179	183	195
	75	153	160	169
	50	121	133	146
	25	87	109	119
	10	64	84	102
6	90	185	195	204
	75	159	166	173
	50	132	145	146
	25	112	116	122
	10	89	91	91

*WCPM = Words Correct Per Minute

Remember, fluent reading is not all about speed. We want students to read at a reasonable rate—a rate that is similar to the speed at which we naturally talk. We don't want speed readers; we want readers who use good expression and can comprehend as they read.

Prosody

Prosody refers to the expression and phrasing students use as they read. It also includes their intonation and volume, and the degree to which they emphasize words and phrases. Unlike accuracy and rate, prosody is much more difficult to measure because it is more subjective. Hudson et al. (2005) developed a checklist to help. Examining the items below can help you understand the multiple components of prosody.

- Student placed vocal emphasis on appropriate words.
- Student's voice tone rose and fell at appropriate points in the text.
- Student's inflection reflected the punctuation in the text (e.g., voice tone rose near the end of a question).
- In narrative text with dialogue, student used appropriate vocal tone to represent characters' mental states, such as excitement, sadness, fear, or confidence.
- Student used punctuation to pause appropriately at phrase boundaries.
- Student used prepositional phrases to pause appropriately at phrase boundaries.
- Student used subject-verb divisions to pause appropriately at phrase boundaries.
- Student used conjunctions to pause appropriately at phrase boundaries.

Instructional Implications

One of the best ways to increase your students' fluency is to engage them in repeated oral reading (The National Reading Panel, 2000). Repeated reading has consistently been reported to be an effective intervention for fluency for beginning readers, as well as students with reading disabilities (Chafouleas et al., 2004). Furthermore, it has been shown to "increase reading rate and accuracy and to transfer to new texts" (Blevins, 2023). Lee and Yoon found that when repeated oral reading was paired with a listening passage preview (i.e., the teacher modeling a fluent reading of the text prior to students' reading of it), the effect was significantly higher (2023). Specifically, they also found that having students repeat a passage four times had a stronger effect than only two or three times. Combining these two interventions (listening passage preview and reading the passage four times) is, according to Lee and Yoon, the most effective method for students with reading difficulties. We can vary the way students read when they read a text multiple times. Using a variety of techniques can increase your students' levels of engagement. Here are three ways:

- Echo Reading: Students hear a model of the text and then repeat what they hear.
- Choral Reading: Students read all together in unison.
- Partner Reading: Students read in pairs.

The Strategies for Success section, starting on page 117, explains how to incorporate these techniques in your practice.

Ways We Overlook Fluency Instruction

It's easy to overlook fluency instruction. We might teach phonics in isolation, expecting students to transfer phonics knowledge on their own, without providing enough opportunities for students to read continuous text. Or we might expect students to increase their fluency by engaging them in round robin reading. Or we might assume that encouraging students to read silently will improve their fluency. These are common mistakes, and it's easy to believe that students will learn to read fluently on their own. However, we must not leave that to chance.

"Students progress at a much faster rate in phonics when the bulk of instructional time is spent on applying the skills to authentic reading and writing experiences, rather than isolated skill-and-drill work."

—Wiley Blevins

Teaching Phonics in Isolation

Teaching phonics explicitly and systematically is very effective, as long as you don't teach it in isolation. Students need plenty of reading practice to internalize the phonics concepts you're teaching. In fact, most of your instructional time should be spent having students apply concepts in authentic reading and writing experiences.

Engaging Students in Round Robin Reading

Many students experience severe anxiety when forced to read aloud. They count ahead paragraphs to see which one they will have to read, and then too often spend time agonizing over the words. They worry about making mistakes and being humiliated in front of their peers. The experience that Ameer Baraka, former inmate and now Emmy-nominated actor/producer, shares is sobering. He says,

> *"I'll never forget when I had to read in sixth grade, and I was called before my English class to read and the teacher simply embarrassed me, because I sit up there for about 10 minutes just floundering through a book not knowing any of the words. And I knew that day I was going to be a dope dealer."* (Farris, 2018)

And that is exactly what happened. He decided to become a drug dealer after the shame he felt when forced to read in front of his class, and he ended up in prison because of that decision. It was while in prison that Baraka was diagnosed with dyslexia and finally got the reading instruction that he needed. He now dedicates his time working on prison reform, dyslexia advocacy, and getting students help before they fail.

Round robin reading is not an effective use of our instructional time. Because only one student reads at a time, while the others supposedly follow along, reading time is extremely limited—maybe one minute per student? That is nowhere near enough practice to improve fluency. And what are the rest of the students doing while a classmate is reading? They are supposed to be paying attention when, in reality, many of them will be off task and unengaged. There are far more worthwhile methods for fluency practice than round robin reading, which I discuss, starting on page 117.

Leaning Too Heavily on Silent Reading

We want our students to become voracious readers who select books to read for pleasure. We might allow considerable time in our classrooms for them to read. However, it would be shortsighted to expect students' oral reading fluency to improve by reading independently and silently. Mark Seidenberg (2018) said, "Children who struggle when reading texts aloud do not become good readers if left to read silently; their dysfluency merely becomes inaudible." Silent reading does not provide the practice students need to develop oral reading fluency.

Proficient readers tend to love independent reading time because they have established the necessary foundational skills to read well. As such, silent reading can "play an important role in improving and strengthening reading (Hasbrouck,

2020)." But what about less proficient readers? Silent reading time can be a waste of time for them. They might stare into space, pretend to read for the benefit of their peers, or take part in some undesirable classroom behaviors. They might be embarrassed to be seen reading the texts that they can be successful with and, instead, choose a text to impress their peers. I vividly remember one of my beginning readers selecting a large chapter book for silent reading time. I knew she lacked the skills to read it, but was surprised by her determination to sit there for the entire 15 minutes pretending to read it. If you provide space for silent reading in your classroom, consider what your struggling readers are doing during that time. We need to become keenly aware of how students are using their time and provide support for those who need it.

In the "reading center," my students have the option to read quietly or listen to audiobooks while I am working with small groups. Listening to audiobooks enables everyone to experience complex texts that build vocabulary and background knowledge. This does not replace opportunities for oral reading practice; I ensure my students have plenty of time for that. But I am absolutely okay with them spending 15 minutes of the day immersed in listening to higher-level texts for enjoyment and content knowledge. Audiobooks are especially important for older students who lack foundational skills. If they are only allowed to read books independently that are on their so-called "level," these students will miss out on so many grade-level concepts and terms. Allowing them to listen to audiobooks means they can access the same content as their classmates. Are the more proficient readers talking about a plot twist in Harry Potter at recess? Audiobooks enable our more fragile learners to join the conversation.

Looking for Popular and Diverse Digital Books? Look No Further Than Epic!

Epic is an online library of popular and diverse books that students can read independently, or you can use for small-group instruction, shared reading, and read-aloud! I love that the text is highlighted while it's being read. Plus, it is free to educators. Go to www.getepic.com to learn more about this fantastic resource.

When he was in third grade, my son with dyslexia was not reading the simple, decodable books his teacher gave him during the class's silent reading time. They embarrassed him, given his peers were reading chapter books. So he was relieved when his teacher, on my suggestion, let him listen to audiobooks, while following along in a print version, during silent reading time. He also continued to receive explicit instruction and oral reading practice, tutoring sessions outside of school, as well as reading with me for 30 minutes every night. The combination of those efforts helped him become the reader he is today. In time, not only did his reading skills grow stronger, but his vocabulary and background knowledge did, too, because of all the exposure he had had to complex text.

Strategies for Success

What follows are some strategies for enhancing your fluency practice.

Remember the Subskills

Remember, fluency is not an isolated skill. There are many underlying skills, or subskills, that need to be addressed for fluency to develop. If your students struggle with fluency, you need to look beyond a fluency score. Do they have a phonemic awareness need? Do they lack sound-symbol knowledge? Do they struggle with automaticity at the letter, letter-pattern, or word level? Do they need more exposure to certain graphemes? Have they had enough meaningful practice opportunities? Once you've gotten to the root of the issue, work on the foundational skills the child needs. At the same time, a weakness in foundational skills does not mean that you need to postpone working on fluency. Instead, integrate fluency practice throughout your reading instruction. For example, as a warm-up to our phonics lesson, I sometimes show alphabet letters to my kindergarteners and have them practice the sound associated with each letter. This develops their automaticity at the letter level. During the lesson, my students might choral-read or partner-read words containing the letter pattern they are learning to develop automaticity at the word level. During small-group time, I might have students read a decodable book several times for different purposes—the first time for accuracy and decoding. For the second read, I might have students focus on reading more smoothly, in addition to accuracy and decoding. For the third read, I might have students continue to work on fluency, while also focusing on the meaning of the text.

Offer Meaningful Practice With Feedback: Small-Group Instruction

Meaningful practice is one of the main goals of my small-group instruction. I aim to maximize the time my students spend in oral reading practice with specific, immediate feedback. To ensure my students get sufficient reading time,

I have all of them read aloud simultaneously during small-group instruction, but individually at various points in the text. This may sound chaotic, but it isn't.

It is important to select texts that are tailored to individual students' needs. Think about skills they need to develop. For example, give decodable passages to groups that are learning phonics patterns to build the automaticity they need. Give more challenging authentic texts to students who are past that stage and have foundational levels of reading accuracy (Hasbrouck, 2020; Adams, 2020). While some of your small groups may be focused on strengthening phonics skills, others may be focused on fluency, vocabulary, and/or comprehension.

Read, Model, Read Again

Drawing on the research from Lee and Yoon (2017) on repeated readings with a teacher preview, along with the techniques by Nora Chahbazi for the EBLI system, I practice this technique with individual students during our small-group time, using both decodable texts and authentic texts:

1. Have your student read aloud a portion of the text—a sentence, a few sentences, a paragraph, or a page.

2. Model-read the same portion of the text for the student, while he tracks the text with a finger.

3. Have the student reread the same portion of text.

Watch a demonstration of Read, Model, Read Again.

This is a simple activity, but so powerful. Students carefully decode words on the initial read. Then they hear a model of fluent, expressive reading by the teacher, listening carefully as they follow along with a finger. Lastly, students get another opportunity to read, which gives them more exposure to the words, develops fluency, and builds confidence.

If I am working with students individually, we often "read, model, read again" every page of the book we are reading. In my classroom, I will do this activity with individual students during our small-group reading time.

Consider the Neurological Impress Method

This method was introduced by Heckelman in 1969, and subsequent research has found it to be effective in developing fluency (Flood et al., 2005). Don't be alarmed by the technical name. The Neurological Impress Method is simply a form of paired reading where the teacher and student read the text aloud at the same time. The teacher should read slightly faster and louder than the student typically reads, while student and teacher track the text with a finger. During small-group time, as I listen to individual students read, I might say, "Now let's read this next page together. Try to keep your voice with mine." I find it useful for students who need a little boost in their reading rate and prosody.

Take Full Advantage of Whole-Group Reading

There are many ways to address fluency in your whole-group instruction. You can:

- read aloud a text, modeling appropriate pacing and prosody, while students follow along with a finger on their own copy.
- do cloze reading, where you pause at words you want students to read, and they read the word.
- do choral reading, where you and students read aloud in unison.
- do echo reading, where you read a short section of the text first (a phrase or sentence), and students repeat it. I find that beginning readers, especially, benefit from this.

All of these techniques are great ways to scaffold instruction, which is necessary when we read more complex text. The level of scaffolding can be faded throughout a lesson or throughout the week. For example, on the first day we read a complex text, I might model read it, while students track the text with a finger. This allows them to hear how one reads at a pace that is suitable for the text and with appropriate phrasing, intonation, and expression. It also allows students to focus on the text's content, and having them track the text with a finger keeps them on task. I may choose to do some cloze and echo reading, too, to give them more practice in accurate and fluent reading. The next day, I might move to choral reading to give everyone an opportunity to practice fluency in a non-threatening way. The third day, I might ask students to read the text in pairs, using some of the partner-reading strategies described on page 122.

Encourage Partner Reading

Partner reading is a wonderful alternative to round robin reading. Not only do students get a lot of reading practice, they also get support and feedback from their partner. They also get support and feedback from you, as you move around the room. Just remember, partner reading should not replace teacher-directed instruction. Students will still need to be explicitly taught new skills before practicing them with their partners.

Abby

Last year, I had a second-grade student, Abby, who was reading just below grade level, at 50 WCPM. (The beginning-of-year benchmark goal is 52 WCPM.) So, I paired her with a slightly stronger reader in hopes that it would help. After a few weeks, I monitored Abby's progress and found that she had made significant gains, reading 64 WCPM. I monitored her progress two weeks later to find that she was at 70 WCPM. At that point, considering Abby's growth, I made her the stronger reader in a new partnership, assigning her to one of my least fluent students. But guess what happened? Two weeks later, I assessed her again and was dismayed to find that her WCPM score had dropped back down to 61. Thankful that I had caught this setback quickly, I paired her with a stronger student, and it made all the difference. In two weeks, her WCPM was back at 70 and continued to improve steadily from there. She ended the year with a very strong score of 121 WCPM, exceeding the end-of-year benchmark goal of 87. This is why it's important to monitor your students' growth regularly and watch for potential stumbling blocks.

Assigning Partners

It's important to be intentional when assigning partners. Rather than letting students choose their partners, match them in a way that will create optimum learning for each. To do that, I suggest pairing low-performing students with average-performing students, and avoid pairing your very strongest readers with your weakest ones. That would frustrate both of them. One way to create these partnerships is to first list your students in order, from least fluent to most fluent. Then split the class in half. Assign the most fluent reader in one half to the most fluent reader in the second half; the second most fluent in one half to the second most fluent in the second half, and so on (Burns et al, 2015). Then look at your pairings and change any that may not work for potential personality and/or behavior issues. Just try to keep reading ability in mind as you make changes.

If you have an odd number of students, you have a couple of options:

1. Assign one of your more fluent readers to be a floater who you can pair with any student whose regular partner is absent.

2. Create a triad. Place one of your less fluent readers with an existing pair. Then make the strongest reader in the trio "Reader 1," who reads first and on his own. When it is "Reader 2's" turn to read, the two remaining students read simultaneously. This provides great support for low-performing students.

I recommend changing pairings about every three to six weeks, or sooner, if there is a problem.

Unquestionably, students should not be told who the weaker and stronger readers are. You can assign them "Reader 1" and "Reader 2" or come up with names for each. In my class, I assign them "Milk" and "Cookie." I've heard other fun names such as Chips and Salsa, Peanut Butter and Jelly, and Ketchup and Mustard. This allows me to give directions easily, such as, "Milks will read first and Cookies follow along with your finger. When my timer goes off, Cookies will read and Milks will follow along." The stronger reader should always begin, to provide a passage preview or model for the other student.

Setting Expectations

We need to think about how we manage partner reading. It's always a good idea to set your expectations right from the beginning. As Anita Archer says, "If you expect it, pre-correct it." So, discuss and practice what effective partner reading looks like and set specific rules. Here are my "5 Easy Rules" (adapted from Fuchs et al., 2008):

Teaching Correction Guidelines

Students will also need correction guidelines so they know what to do when their partner misreads or struggles with a word. I encourage my students to take on the role of "coach" or "supporter" in order to be ready to help their partners when necessary. I also encourage them to use Archer's (2011) "Ask, Then Tell" procedure: When the coach or supporter hears the reader read a word incorrectly, she points to the word and asks, "Can you figure out this word?" Then she waits four seconds, and if the reader hasn't responded, the coach says, "This word is _____. What word?" The reader says the word. Then the coach or supporter says, "Now reread the sentence."

To help your students learn this procedure, share this video with them.

Partner Reading
5 Easy Rules

1. Talk only to your partner and only about your reading.
2. Keep your voices low.
3. Cooperate with your partner.
4. Try your best.
5. Follow directions.

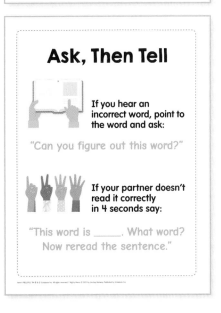

Ask, Then Tell

If you hear an incorrect word, point to the word and ask:

"Can you figure out this word?"

If your partner doesn't read it correctly in 4 seconds say:

"This word is _____. What word? Now reread the sentence."

Try "Me We Reading"

This is an excellent strategy that I learned from Archer and Hughes's *Explicit Instruction* (2011). I think this is best used as a partner-reading activity. Have students read aloud in pairs, and take turns on each page. Before reading, Partner 1 tells her partner whether she chooses "me" or "we." If the student chooses "me," then she reads the page aloud independently while her partner follows along with his finger. If the student chooses "we," then both partners read aloud the page together. On the next page, Partner 2 gets to choose "me" or "we." I created a video of this strategy to use in my classroom as a way to introduce it. You are welcome to use it in yours and can find it here.

Choosing Your Procedure

You can structure partner-reading procedures in many ways. You could assign each student a certain amount of text to read before switching. For example, they can switch off every other sentence, paragraph, or page.

Another way is to use the Me We Reading technique described to the left. Students could alternate pages, and when it's their turn, choose "me" or "we."

Another way is to assign an amount of time. For example, "Milk will read for four minutes and Cookie will follow along. When my timer goes off, it's Cookie's turn. They will go back to the beginning and read for four minutes." For a very specific protocol for partner reading that I've had great success with, see page 123.

Partner reading is such an effective use of class time. It provides students with so many practice opportunities—and it tends to keep all students on-task because they are actively engaged in reading. I always monitor students as they read by walking around the room and giving constructive feedback. This activity can be scaffolded by model-reading the text aloud earlier in the week, as well as choral-reading it with the entire class. These techniques support students as they move toward reading grade-level text independently and proficiently.

Partner Reading Paragraph Shrinking

Partner Reading Paragraph Shrinking is an evidence-based activity based on Peer Assisted Learning Strategies (PALS; Fuchs et al., 2001) and modified by Burns et al. (2015), recommended for Grades 2–8. After watching a presentation by Dr. Burns, and learning about the activity's almost immediate, positive effects, I was eager to try it out in my classroom. Over half of my second-grade students were starting the year below grade level benchmark goals, with a class median WCPM of 50. After only two weeks of implementing Partner Reading Paragraph Shrinking, that median rose to 64 WCPM! I was immediately hooked. Over the year, the activity consistently improved the reading proficiency of my students. By the end of the year, my class median was 118 WCPM, well over the benchmark of 87 WCPM. Here are the steps:

See my PaTTAN presentation on Partner Reading Paragraph Shrinking.

- Pair up your students as described on page 120.
- Give each student a folder with the procedures, passages on the weaker reader's instructional level, error correction handout, and paragraph shrinking instructions.
- Have students meet for 20 minutes a day for two weeks.
- On the first day, explain the set-up procedures, the rules, and correction guidelines. Then have students practice: Reader 1 reads for 5 minutes while Reader 2 follows along; then Reader 2 goes back to the beginning and reads for 5 minutes while Reader 1 follows along.
- On the second day, teach and model Paragraph Shrinking, a three-step process to help students summarize each paragraph (see page 149). Students identify who or what the paragraph is about, say the most important idea about the "who" or "what," and then say the main idea in 10 words or less. Then have students practice: Reader 1 reads for 5 minutes, stopping to summarize after every paragraph; then Reader 2 continues reading wherever Reader 1 left off for 5 minutes, stopping to summarize after every paragraph.
- Continue the activity for days 2 to 10. (Extend the activity longer if you desire.)
    - Reader 1 reads the text for 5 minutes.
    - Reader 2 reads the same text for 5 minutes.
    - Reader 1 continues reading where Reader 2 left off, stopping to summarize after every paragraph.
    - Reader 2 continues reading where Reader 1 left off, stopping to summarize after every paragraph.

Download all the handouts for partner reading.

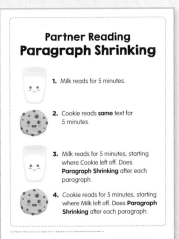

Partner Reading
Paragraph Shrinking

1. Milk reads for 5 minutes.

2. Cookie reads **same** text for 5 minutes.

3. Milk reads for 5 minutes, starting where Cookie left off. Does **Paragraph Shrinking** after each paragraph.

4. Cookie reads for 5 minutes, starting where Milk left off. Does **Paragraph Shrinking** after each paragraph.

Rehearse and Perform Texts

An authentic way to give students repeated reading practice is to have them rehearse and perform a text for an audience. Using Reader's Theater scripts, speeches, or poems is an enjoyable and invigorating way for students to improve their reading fluency. Preparing for a performance is an authentic reason for students to read a text multiple times, and is effective in developing prosody.

My students keep poetry folders, to which we add a new poem each week. Every Monday, I read that poem aloud while students follow along. Throughout the week, we read the poem by echo reading, cloze reading, and choral reading before moving to partner reading. This is a great activity when we have a few extra minutes at any point of the day. Students also read the poem at the reading center. On Fridays, students volunteer to perform the poem—and almost all of them do! I group them so that everyone gets the opportunity to perform, without taking too much time.

Scoop Phrases

Phrase scooping is a way of chunking text into meaningful units by drawing scoops under groups of words that naturally go together. That means chunking where there are pauses, intonation changes, or emphasis changes intended by the writer of the text. It encourages students to read by phrases instead of

word by word, which can lead to better comprehension. "Good readers make meaning by reading in phrases; struggling readers limit meaning by reading word by word (Ellery et al., 2015)."

Practice Timed Repeated Reading

Timed Repeated Reading (Hudson et al., 2022) is similar in some ways to assessing WCPM. However, it is not used as an assessment but as a way to improve the student's reading fluency. It is designed to be used as an intervention, one-on-one, for slow but accurate readers, and not for those who are already fluent. I find that it's best to use this intervention in Grades 2 and up.

Hudson and colleagues (2022) recommend doing Timed Repeated Reading for 5 to 15 minutes at least three times a week in order to provide enough sustained practice. It can be used at the letter, word, or text level. If the student is unable to name at least 60 correct letter sounds per minute with two or fewer mistakes, start with the letter and word level. Otherwise, choose a passage between 50 and 200 words that the student can read with at least 90 percent accuracy. Choosing the right passage is the key to the student's motivation (Hudson et al., 2022). See the steps below.

Timed Repeated Readings Cycle

1. Preview Material
2. Set Goals and Review Graph
3. Read and Record for 1 Minute
4. Provide Constructive Feedback
5. Calculate Score
6. Graph Data
7. Repeat steps 3-6
8. Analyze Trends and Check Goals
9. Celebrate and Support!

1. **Preview Material** Let the student practice reading the passage before being timed. Encourage her to practice reading the text accurately. Model correct pronunciations of words or sounds that may be difficult for the student.

2. **Set Goals and Review Graph** Have the student review her WCPM graph from previous sessions and set a goal for the current session. For example, the goal might be to read five more words in one minute. The student may also have an overarching goal that she is hoping to reach by the end of the week or a specified amount of time. Keep the discussion positive, aiming to encourage and motivate the child.

3. **Read and Record for One Minute**
Have the student read aloud for one minute, keeping your timer out of the view of the student. As the student reads, mark any errors. If she pauses and doesn't know the word, tell it to her and count it as an error. Wait only 3 seconds before providing the word so as not to inhibit her momentum.

4. **Provide Constructive Feedback** Offer praise and advice. Give time for the student to practice any corrections.

5. **Calculate Score** Subtract the number of errors from the total number of words read in one minute. This will give you the WCPM score.

6. **Graph Data** Help the student fill out the graph to represent the WCPM score.

7. **Repeat Steps 3–6** Time the student for one minute as she reads aloud the same passage again. Repeating Step 3 gives the student another opportunity to practice and a chance to improve her score. While Hudson and colleagues don't include this step, I find it motivates students because they almost always do better on the second read. Calculate and graph the data once again.

Download blank fluency record-keeping form.

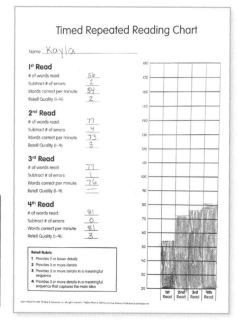

8. **Analyze Trends and Check Goals** Check your student's goals and any trends you might notice. The student should achieve both rate and accuracy goals before moving on to a new passage. If the rate is not improving, consider what adjustments may need to be made. For example, sometimes I have the student practice reading the passage aloud simultaneously with me as part of Step 1.

9. **Celebrate and Support!** Celebrate and congratulate students when they meet or get close to their goals. Set future goals for things they need to work on.

Timing this intervention keeps the data consistent. If you are concerned about the pressure timed reading can put on students, I believe that how you frame it will directly impact how the student feels about the activity. Keep your attitude relaxed, and not frantic. Place the timer out of view of the student and make sure you have appropriate, realistic goals. My intervention students love trying to beat their scores and are motivated when they get to color in their graphs to track their progress. But always consider your students, and if the timed reading stresses them out, alter the activity so that it is both positive and effective for them. You might choose a set amount of the passage (e.g., the first two paragraphs) for them to read untimed, and then calculate and graph how many words they are able to read correctly within that portion of the text.

In Closing, Remember...

- Fluency has a direct impact on students' comprehension.
- When students are not fluent and have to focus intensely on retrieving sound-symbol correspondences from memory, they do not have much cognitive space left to think about what they are reading.
- Systematic and explicit phonics is effective as long as it is not taught in isolation. Students need plenty of opportunities to read continuous text to internalize the phonics concepts we teach.
- Round robin reading creates an unnecessary emotional toll on students that can lead to devastating effects. It is an ineffective practice and has extremely limited practice opportunities for students.
- Students who struggle to read texts orally do not become good readers if left to read silently.
- Fluency is a complex skill that requires students to read accurately, with appropriate rate and expression, to make meaning.
- Accuracy, rate, and prosody remain the cornerstones of fluency.
- We must address the foundational subskills of reading, so that fluency can evolve from there.
- Research has consistently found that repeated oral reading is effective for developing fluency.
- Students must have multiple, meaningful practice opportunities to improve fluency.
- Choral reading, cloze reading, echo reading, partner reading, performing, text scooping, and timed repeated reading are effective techniques for improving fluency.

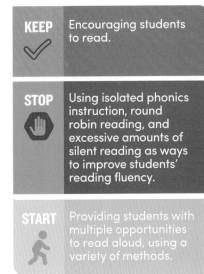

KEEP Encouraging students to read.

STOP Using isolated phonics instruction, round robin reading, and excessive amounts of silent reading as ways to improve students' reading fluency.

START Providing students with multiple opportunities to read aloud, using a variety of methods.

Improve Comprehension by Developing Vocabulary and Background Knowledge

I am a proficient reader, but if I were given a text on chemical engineering, I would have an extremely difficult time comprehending it, mainly because I lack the necessary background knowledge and vocabulary. I would be overwhelmed by unfamiliar words and concepts. Researchers have known for years that the most important factor in good reading comprehension is how much vocabulary and background knowledge the reader has on the subject (Hirsch, 2003; Shapiro, 2004). Sometimes we work so hard teaching our students word-recognition skills that we neglect other key areas. But it is important to remember the upper strands of Hollis Scarborough's Reading Rope, shown on page 9.

Reading Comprehension Explained

Reading comprehension is complex. It is not a single "skill," but an "orchestrated product of a set of linguistic and cognitive processes" (Castles et al., 2018). While the word-recognition strands of the Reading Rope tend to get significant attention in the primary grades, the language-comprehension strands are also critical and need to be taught as well: background knowledge, vocabulary, language structures, verbal reasoning, and literacy knowledge. All of those elements, combined with strong oral language skills, contribute to our language comprehension.

Reading comprehension differs from language comprehension because of its reliance on print. Students need to be able to read a text's words accurately and fluently to comprehend that text. Dr. Anita Archer wisely cautioned, "There is no comprehension strategy powerful enough to compensate for the fact that you can't read the words" (2011). The foundational skills of reading are essential and must be taught for students to become proficient readers who can comprehend as they read.

In addition to word recognition, fluency and language comprehension, students with good reading comprehension use cognitive strategies such as monitoring,

> While the word-recognition strands of the Reading Rope tend to get significant attention in the primary grades, the language-comprehension strands are also critical and need to be taught as well.

questioning, and summarizing (Berkeley et al., 2009). This helps them focus on the text's critical content. Skilled comprehenders also use inferences and their knowledge of text structure to construct a representation of the text's meaning (Cain, 2009).

So, as you can see, reading comprehension is much more complicated than one might think. There is no question that there are many factors that contribute to it, but vocabulary and background knowledge are especially critical (Catts et al., 2016; Smith et al., 2021).

I experienced this firsthand when my son asked me to select a book on black holes to read together. As we read, I found myself having to stop, reread, and reread again. I struggled to comprehend the text and had to look up meanings of words such as *quasars* and *event horizon*. My son, however, had already built up quite a bit of content knowledge on this subject. He was able to extract

meaning from the text much more easily than I was, and was building on his knowledge of the subject, while I struggled to understand the very basics! Even though I am a more proficient reader, he was comprehending much better than me.

The "Baseball Study" (Recht & Leslie, 1988) illustrates that point. In the study, the researchers divided students into groups based on members' reading ability and knowledge of baseball. After students read a passage about baseball, they answered a series of comprehension questions. The researchers found that the students with low reading ability but a high level of baseball knowledge outperformed the students with high reading ability but low knowledge of baseball. Background knowledge matters.

However, many reading programs neglect it by focusing too much on skills and strategy. According to Timothy Shanahan, "Too often the emphasis of a reading lesson is so much on the reading skill or strategy that the opportunity to expand children's understanding of their world is lost." (2017) Natalie Wexler (2020) also talks about this in *The Knowledge Gap*. Teaching comprehension skills such as "compare and contrast" do not necessarily lead to improved comprehension. So instead of focusing so much of our attention on them, we need to build students' vocabulary and background knowledge. It's important to realize that comprehension is an outcome and not a skill to be taught.

Instructional Implications

In this section, I discuss the cornerstones of reading comprehension: background knowledge and vocabulary.

Background Knowledge

We can begin building background knowledge from the time students enter kindergarten. Reading aloud helps them learn new things, think critically, and see a variety of perspectives. Providing a rich mix of powerful books engages them and prepares them to tackle complex texts themselves. Having rich conversations about those books expands their oral language, vocabulary, and thinking skills.

Using a reading curriculum that develops knowledge is ideal. If the curriculum you're required to use focuses more on comprehension skills than knowledge, find ways to bring in content to build students' background knowledge, such as adding topic-related texts to a unit. Explicitly teach facts that relate to the text before having students read it. And don't forget to front-load vocabulary words that students will encounter as they read the text.

Deepen Knowledge Through Writing Instruction

One of the best ways to deepen students' knowledge is by having them write about what they read. Research by Graham, Harris, and Santangelo (2015) shows that when elementary-grade students do that, rather than simply reading and rereading the text, their comprehension jumps by 24 percentile points. Writing and content knowledge have a reciprocal relationship. It's difficult to write about a topic you don't know much about. At the same time, if you build background knowledge about that topic by reading, writing about it becomes easier and deepens understanding of it.

Hochman & Wexler (2017) recommend having students practice writing about content-area topics as soon as possible, which provides a wonderful opportunity to boost their learning. In their book, *The Writing Revolution*, they present practical ideas for teaching a variety of writing skills using the content you are covering in other subjects. It is an excellent resource.

The Benefits of Read-Aloud

- Improves listening skills.
- Builds language comprehension.
- Introduces students to new concepts and ideas.
- Boosts vocabulary.
- Teaches language structure.
- Cultivates a love for reading.

"Writing about content helps students clarify and organize their thoughts, solidify the material they are learning, and place that learning into their long-term memory."

—Joan Sedita

Vocabulary

According to Hennessy, "There is no lack of evidence for the importance of vocabulary knowledge in developing skilled reading" (2020). Students not only need to understand the meanings of words, but also the relationships between words and the context in which the words appear to enhance their comprehension (Kame'enui & Baumann, 2012).

While students will learn many words incidentally when reading, talking, and listening, many other words need to be directly and explicitly taught. When teachers intentionally teach target words before students encounter them in a text, students' comprehension of the text improves, as well as their comprehension of the words themselves (McKeown et al., 1985; Stahl & Fairbanks, 1986).

We know how important vocabulary knowledge is, but what is the best way to teach it? According to McKeown (2019), there is strong consensus from decades of research on the features of effective instruction. Those features include providing a definition, multiple encounters with the word in multiple contexts, and opportunities for students to interact with the word to deepen their knowledge of its meaning, uses, and connections to other words. Specifically, research suggests that 12 encounters help to increase reading comprehension (McKeown et al., 1985). Additionally, Elleman and colleagues recommend high levels of discussion to promote vocabulary development (2009).

Ways Students Can Write About Their Reading

- Personal reactions to the text
- Analysis and interpretation of it
- Summary of it
- Notes about it
- Questions and answers about it

(Graham & Hebert, 2010)

What Words Should We Teach?

Beck and colleagues (2013) divide words into three categories:

- **Tier 1:** common words that are used frequently in everyday conversations (e.g., *happy, house*)
- **Tier 2:** sophisticated, wide-ranging, high-utility words that are less likely than Tier 1 words to be learned independently (e.g., *fortunate, relieved*)
- **Tier 3:** words that are limited to specific domains and not encountered frequently (e.g., *cardiovascular, ecosystem*)

They recommend focusing instruction on Tier 2 words, which students encounter often in their reading. They also recommend selecting words that are not too difficult to explain to younger students. Furthermore, they recommend choosing words that are critical to understanding the text's meaning, words that are useful to students now and in the future, and words with multiple meanings. They also recommend words with semantic relatives and morphological families that will support the growth of more words. Limit the number of words you teach in a lesson to 4 or 5 and provide multiple experiences with those words throughout the week. Teaching Tier 3 words in content-area lessons is an important way to build knowledge in science, social studies, and other domains. Overall, Beck and colleagues state, "Teachers should feel free to use their best judgment, based on an understanding of their students' needs, in selecting words to teach."

The Right Amount of Strategy Instruction

While it's best to devote a lot of your teaching time to vocabulary and background knowledge, some strategy instruction is beneficial. The National Reading Panel (2000) found that teaching certain strategies did improve students' reading comprehension, including recall, generating and asking questions, and summarizing texts. Its report recommends instruction that encourages flexible-use strategies so students know when to use a specific strategy. According to the report, "Multiple-strategy instruction that is flexible as to which strategies are used and when they are taught over the course of a reading session provides a natural basis for teachers and readers to interact over texts."

Additionally, Berkeley et al. (2009) found the use of cognitive strategies, which include activating background knowledge, self-monitoring, self-questioning, and summarizing, is very effective. Instruction in these strategies consistently improves students' ability to notice relationships in stories, ask and answer deep questions about the text, and offer more focused retellings. Key to that instruction's success are careful and precise teacher modeling of each strategy, and monitoring of students' use of each one.

Palinscar and Brown's Reciprocal Teaching, a scaffolded discussion technique, is one such approach to instruction (1984), which is based on four strategies: asking questions, summarizing, predicting, and clarifying. The teacher models her use of each strategy by thinking aloud while reading and allowing practice and discussion of each one. Depending on the ages and developmental levels of the students, the strategies can be introduced one at a time or all together. Eventually, students can take turns "being the teacher" by modeling each strategy in small groups.

Strategies for Success

Here are some practical strategies for improving comprehension instruction, organized into the three categories: strategies for developing vocabulary and background knowledge simultaneously, strategies for developing vocabulary, and strategies for developing and activating background knowledge.

Strategies for Developing Vocabulary and Background Knowledge Simultaneously

Implement a Routine for Oral Language

Oral language provides the foundation for literacy. I recently learned about a daily routine (Carreker, 2003) that expands students' vocabulary and background knowledge, and strengthens their writing skills (Peck, 2022), and it takes just 5–10 minutes a day. Here are the steps:

DAY 1: NAMING

Have students name items starting with a broad topic (e.g., clothing, furniture, pets, animals, transportation) and then narrow their choices (e.g., clothing you wear in the summer, clothing you wear in the winter). Be sure to keep this activity oral. Don't write anything down just yet, but do scaffold your instruction by providing some pictures for the students (e.g., display an image of a hot summer day and a cold, winter day).

DAY 2: DESCRIBING

Hold up an item or a picture of the item and ask students to describe it following this structure: name the object (e.g., a scarf), the categories it might fit in (e.g., clothing, winter clothes, things you can knit, things that are soft), sensory details about the item based on prompts you give them (e.g., What does a scarf feel like? What color is it? What is it used for?). Repeat the process with a second object if you have time (e.g., a mitten).

DAY 3: LISTENING AND ANSWERING QUESTIONS

To build students' listening comprehension, read aloud a related text to the class (e.g., *The Mitten* by Jan Brett) and then ask students questions at the end (e.g., Why did the grandma want the boy to have red mittens? How did the boy lose his mitten? What happened next?).

DAY 4: RETELLING

Model how to retell the story and have students retell it to a partner.

DAY 5: WRITING

Ask students to write a paragraph with a prompt that relates to the topic of the week (e.g., describe a mitten).

Download blank oral language unit planner.

Here's an example of days 1–4 of this routine (Peck, 2022):

Sample Oral Language Unit	
Unit 3: Animals	
Day 1/Activity: **Naming**	Teacher leads students through naming animals: **1.** Let's name animals. **2.** Let's name animals that we see on a farm. **3.** Let's name animals that we see in the zoo. **4.** Let's name animals that live in the jungle. **5.** Let's name animals that live in the ocean.
Day 2/Activity: **Describing**	(Teacher needs pictures of a horse and a zebra) First, the teacher shows a picture of a horse and leads students through the discussion that includes: **1.** Name of animal **2.** Categories/groups that a horse belongs in (farm animals, work animals, animals you can ride, etc.) **3.** Function of a horse — what is it used for? (riding, farm work, etc.) **4.** Color **5.** Size **6.** Then, the teacher shows the picture of a zebra and asks students to compare the horse to the zebra. Students compare the colors, sizes, and functions of these two animals.
Day 3/Activity: **Listening to a Story and Answering Questions**	(Teacher needs pictures of a snake, bird, rabbit, and puppy) The teacher reads a story entitled *Abdul's Birthday Present* from the manual and uses the pictures as an anchor chart for students and then asks simple and complex questions about the story. Teacher may ask students to answer in complete sentences, perhaps using sentence stems that a student can complete if necessary.
Day 4/Activity: **Retelling the Story**	**1.** The teacher models the retelling of *Abdul's Birthday Present*, using the pictures from the prior day and complete sentences. **2.** Students retell the story with a partner. **3.** Students take turns retelling the story at least two more times as a whole class, with a different partner or with the teacher.

Find more lessons like these in *The Colors & Shapes of Language: Developing Oral Language & Listening Comprehension* by Neuhaus Education Center.

Give Rich Read-Alouds

Rich read-alouds are essential in building comprehension. Select complex texts above students' current grade level to build oral language skills, as well as their knowledge and vocabulary. Introduce them to new books, favorite books, classic literature, and high-quality informational texts, in a variety of genres and by a variety of authors. It's important for students to experience diverse books that represent a variety of cultural backgrounds. "Choosing texts that have rich ideas and sophisticated themes can help students build world and word knowledge to support future reading." (Cervetti & Hiebert, 2018) Consider enhancing your read-alouds with explicit vocabulary instruction and pre-planned questions to deepen students' experience with the text.

Text Talk is an approach to read-alouds designed to enhance children's ability to construct meaning (Beck & McKeown, 2001), as well as their vocabulary, using open-ended questions to encourage meaningful discussions. It can be time-consuming to select texts, choose vocabulary words, and create questions ourselves, so I was delighted to find a resource filled with teacher-created Text Talk lessons.

Download Text Talk lessons.

Offer Multiple Texts on the Same Topic

Start with one excellent text on a topic you're exploring and then add texts on the same topic to deepen students' knowledge and vocabulary acquisition. Consider the content area standards for your grade level and create text sets that address those standards.

I use the "Article-a-Day" resource by ReadWorks to create text sets. I can browse suggested monthly topics and print out 5 or 6 articles on that topic. I then have students read the texts in pairs to provide meaningful fluency practice and to support their comprehension using paragraph shrinking. (See page 149 for more on paragraph shrinking.)

Provide a Wide Range of Reading Opportunities

The more students read, the more they learn. They learn about our world, consider new perspectives, and gain new insights. We want our proficient readers spending time reading a variety of texts independently. If students are not reading independently, we can provide learning opportunities through read-alouds, shared reading, and audiobooks. Technology, such as audiobooks, allows older students who continue to struggle to access grade-level content and sophisticated vocabulary. According to Hennessy, "Encounters with new words in varied texts have the potential for improving vocabulary whether students read with their eyes or ears" (2020).

Additionally, we can scaffold complex text for students by using structured shared reading strategies such as echo reading, choral reading, and partner reading, which allow them to examine texts more closely and joyfully, with our support. They give students an opportunity to practice decoding and fluency skills, read for meaning, connect background knowledge and new information, and improve their vocabulary. Providing a wide variety of texts, both fiction and nonfiction, for our students to read independently as well as with our support helps them to expand and develop their content knowledge.

Encourage Keyword Outlines

Creating a keyword outline is a technique I learned from the Institute for Excellence in Writing.

- Provide a short text (i.e., about six sentences long) to students. Read aloud the text to students and then read it all together.
- Identify three key words in each sentence. For example, read the first sentence to the students and ask, "What do you think are the three most important words in this sentence?" Have students discuss possible choices with a partner, and then discuss them as a class.
- Have students circle the three words they chose. Then repeat the process for the rest of the sentences.

What a Fox Eats

A fox sometimes hunts for insects. He also likes lizards and mice. He sneaks up quietly and pounces on his prey. Sometimes he steals eggs to eat. He also eats his fruits and vegetables. The fox likes a healthy diet.

Name: Aubrey

Student Handout 7.5
Key Word Outline Portfolio Page

What a Fox Eats

1. sometimes, hunts, insects
1. lizards, mice
1. sneaks, pounces, prey
1. steals, eggs, eat
1. eats, fruits, vegetables
6. likes, healthy, diet

Name: Aubrey

Student Handout 7.6
Portfolio Page

What a fox Eats
Foxes enjoy lizards and mice.
Foxes sometimes hunt insects.
They sneak up on their prey.
Then they pounce on the prey.
They steal eggs to eat. They
eat fruit and vegetables. They
like a healthy diet.

© Institute for Excellence in Writing.
Used by permission of IEW.

- Create a keyword outline with these words. To do that, start by having students put the topic of the passage at the top of a sheet of paper. Under that, have them put a Roman numeral 1 and write the three words from the first sentence. These words will be part of the topic sentence.

- Underneath those three words, have students write numbers 1–5, one line for each of the remaining sentences of the text, and write the three words they circled for each sentence on each line. These will be the supporting details of the paragraph they write. Have students put away the original text so they don't copy it.

- The next part is one of my favorites! Have students orally create sentences from each line of key words. This encourages them to attend to meaning and develops their knowledge of syntax and semantics.

- Have them use the outline to compose a paragraph. I find this is an excellent way to support students' comprehension and writing skills.

As students become comfortable with the process, introduce longer texts from which they choose around six interesting or relevant facts that they want to write about.

7 MIGHTY MOVES

Practice Sentence-Level Instruction

Comprehension instruction can start at the sentence level. By teaching students how to write more complex sentences, we prepare them to understand complex sentences that they encounter in their reading. Reading and writing are, after all, reciprocal processes. You can weave all kinds of sentence-level activities throughout the day. Here are a couple of my favorites:

SENTENCE COMBINING

One of the most powerful strategies for writing instruction is sentence combining (Graham & Perin, 2007; Hochman & Wexler, 2017). In this strategy, students are given short declarative sentences and find ways to combine them into longer, more complex sentences. I usually choose two sentences from a grade-level text that we are reading and write them on the board. Then I walk students through a sentence-combining process that comes from Dr. Deborah Glaser's Top Ten Tools professional training.

1. **Read the two sentences aloud to students and ask them what the relationship is between them.** Are they about the same idea? Does the second sentence extend an idea from the first one? Or does the second sentence move in a different direction? In other words, do they contain contrasting ideas? Does one sentence explain the other?

2. **List possible joining words that reflect the sentences' relationship.** For example, if the sentences are both about the same idea, and the second one extends the idea in the first, you might list these words: *and*, *in addition*, or *also*. If the two sentences contain contrasting ideas, you might list these words: *but*, *yet*, *however*, or *although*. If the sentences have a cause-and-effect relationship, you might list these words: *because*, *since*, *therefore*, or *so*.

3. **If students are new to the process, model how to combine the sentences using one of the joining words.**

4. **Give students time to decide how they might combine the two sentences, using the possible joining words that you listed.** Allow time for them to rehearse their sentences orally with a partner. Walk around to listen and give feedback.

5. **Discuss with students the many possible ways they could combine the sentences.** Have a few students recite their combined sentences, as you write a few of them on the board.

6. **Have students write down their sentences while you walk around and provide help as needed.**

Students may need scaffolding with this activity at first. With my first graders, I spend several lessons combining sentences with the words *and* or *also* before moving on to sentences with the words *but* or *however*. Don't rush the process, and do provide as much help as students need.

Sentence Combining: An Example

After reading a story with my class, I wrote the following two sentences on the board:

Rubina was invited to a party.

Sana was not invited.

Next, we discussed the relationship between these sentences. They are both about a party, but one girl was invited while the other was not, so these are contrasting ideas. I listed possible joining words on the board: *but, yet, however, although*. After allowing some time to think, students discussed with their partners ways to combine the sentences:

Rubina was invited to a party, but Sana was not.

Rubina was invited to a party, however Sana was not.

Although Rubina was invited to the party, Sana was not.

Sana was not invited to the party, however Rubina was invited.

From there, we discussed their possibilities as a class. Finally, students wrote their preferred sentence in their notebooks.

ADDING RELATIVE CLAUSES

My second graders' reading comprehension and writing skills blossomed when I taught how to add a relative clause, beginning with the words *who* or *which*, to combine sentences. Most of them could do this independently and would include relative clauses in their own writing. They could also point out relative clauses when they encountered them in books. As with basic sentence combining described earlier, teaching this process takes a lot of modeling, scaffolding, and practice, but it's worth it. I start with simple sentences from texts we're reading in class or adapt sentences if the text we're reading is complex, such as:

Rex is a big dog.

Rex likes to chase the ball.

Model for students how you can combine these sentences with the word *who*.

Rex, who is a big dog, likes to chase the ball.

Here's another example, using the word *which*:

She put on her sweater.

The sweater was soft and warm.

Combined sentence: She put on her sweater, which was soft and warm.

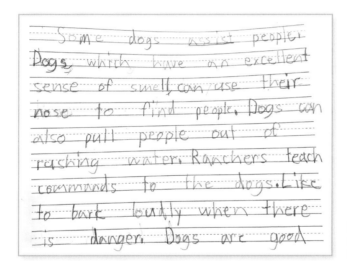

Here's how one of my students included a relative clause in his writing.

Strategies for Developing Vocabulary

Implement an Instructional Routine for Vocabulary

After using various vocabulary routines, I was reintroduced to this one in a training by Dr. Anita L. Archer. You can also find it in *Explicit Instruction: Effective and Efficient Teaching*, the book she wrote with Dr. Charles A. Hughes (2011). I love the simplicity and straight-forwardness of this routine. Archer is a master of effective vocabulary instruction, and I recommend watching online videos of her teaching this process.

Vocabulary Instructional Routine
1. Introduce the word's pronunciation.
2. Introduce the word's meaning.
3. Illustrate the word with examples (and non-examples, when helpful).
4. Check students' understanding.

1. **Introduce the word and its pronunciation.**
   - Display the word and have the students repeat it.
   - Have students tap, clap, or pound the syllables of the word.

        This word is *scamper*. What word? *scamper*.

        Tap and say the parts: *scam-per*.

        Again: *scam-per*.

        scamper is a verb, an action word.

2. **Present a student-friendly definition.**
   - Tell students the definition or have them read it with you.

        scamper means to run with short, small steps.

3. **Illustrate the word with examples:**
   - Concrete examples (act it out or use an object)
   - Visual examples
   - Verbal examples

        When you scamper, you run quickly with short, small steps.
        (Use fingers to imitate short, small steps running across the palm
        of your other hand.)

These mice scamper
across the floor.

The kids scampered out
to the playground.

4. **Check students' understanding, using one of these options:**
   - Ask deep-processing questions:

     Why might a mouse scamper across the floor?

     Begin by saying: A mouse might scamper across the floor because...
   - Have students discern between non-examples and examples:

     Tell me *scamper* or *not scamper*.

     A squirrel finds a nut and quickly runs to hide it. (Scamper)

     An elephant slowly walks over to the watering hole. (Not scamper)
   - Have students compare the word to other words:

     Last week we learned the word *sprint*. How are *scamper* and *sprint* similar? How are they different? Let's compare the words *scampered* and *scampering*. How are they similar? How are they different?

Teach Three-Column Notes

Three-Column Notes come from Dr. Deborah Glaser's Top Ten Tools professional training. It is one of my favorite ways to introduce words and provide multiple exposures to them throughout the week.

Download blank template for three-column notes.

1. Have students fold a sheet of paper into three columns or provide a blackline master of the image on the next page.

2. Have them write the target word in the first column, write a student-friendly definition in the second column, and draw a picture that illustrates the word in the third column.

3. Have students fold the picture column back so it's directly behind the definition column. Then fold the first column back so it's on top of the picture column. Students should now see the column of words on one side and the column definitions on the other.

4. Have them stand up, push in their chairs, and walk around the room until you say stop. You could play music while they're walking around.

5. When the music stops, or when you say stop, have each student buddy-up with a classmate nearby. Ask one partner to choose a word from the first column and the other partner to give the definition. An alternative is to have them use the word in a sentence, instead of giving the definition. Have them check their responses by referring to their notes and then switch roles.

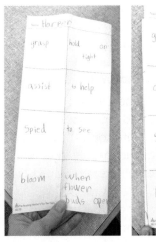

6. Have them continue to quiz each other until the music starts again, or you say go. They walk around again and repeat the process.

This activity can be done throughout the week as a fun way to review the week's vocabulary words.

Perform Vocabulary Skits

Students love to act out vocabulary words. Recent research shows that physically performing an action to represent a word leads to enhanced memory of it (Roberts et al., 2022). My students love coming up with actions for our vocabulary words. They also love performing vocabulary skits. Here are the steps:

1. Divide students into small groups and give each group an index card with 2 or 3 vocabulary words on it. Make sure you have already explicitly taught the words on the cards.

2. Give groups about 5–10 minutes to create a short skit in which they must use all the words on the card. Monitor the groups to ensure they are using their time wisely and using the target words correctly.

3. Have students perform their skits for the class. As each group performs, have audience members listen for the vocabulary words. Afterward, have them share the words they heard.

Model Academic Language

One of the best ways I know to get students to use academic language in their speaking and writing is by using it myself in conversations with them. Find ways to incorporate sophisticated words throughout your day. For example, instead of asking students, "Please get out your 'big books'," I say, "Please get out your anthologies." I remember the first time I did that the students looked around the room, clearly perplexed. I explained, "An anthology is a collection of stories. Can you get out your anthology so we can find our story in it and read it?" Not long afterward, students were using "anthology" themselves. Another time, my second-grade class was watching a step-by-step instructional video to complete an art project. At one point, I paused the video to allow a student to catch up and was delighted when he said, "Okay, you can resume the video now." I was impressed with his accurate and spontaneous use of the word *resume*. Lane and Allen (2010) encourage us to elevate the language we use with students in order to enhance their vocabulary. In the chart below, they share many sophisticated words you can add at different points in the day.

Sophisticated Words to Use During Classroom Routines					
Classroom Supplies		Walking in Line		Group Time	
accumulate	distribute	adjacent	perpendicular	articulate	disperse
allocate	dole	approach	proceed	ascertain	elaborate
allot	gather	disorderly	procession	assemble	elucidate
amass	hoard	efficiently	proximity	coherent	express
arrange	issue	file	queue	contribute	lucid
collect	replenish	halt	rapidly	converse	oblige
deplete	reserve	linger	swiftly	convey	partake
dispense	stockpile	orderly	vicinity	cooperate	participate
		parallel	vicinity	deliberate	portray
		pause		determine	verbalize
				disband	

Sophisticated Words to Use When Discussing Classroom Behavior or Performance

Satisfactorily	Conflict	Impolite	Correct	Wrong
affable	amends	boorish	accomplished	awkward
agreeable	bicker	coarse	appropriate	erroneous
amiable	quarrel	discourteous	exemplary	flawed
compassionate	rectify	offensive	masterful	inaccurate
considerate	resolve	uncouth	precise	inadequate
courteous	squabble	vulgar	proficient	incorrect
decorous			proper	invalid
gracious			superior	
pleasant			suitable	
respectful				
sympathetic				

Sophisticated Words That Relate to Specific Content Areas

Science: Plant Life		Science: Space		Social Studies: Civilizations	
abundant	meandering	celestial	orb	cooperation	obligation
burgeoning	neglect	existence	remote	customary	prosperity
dwindling	sow	globe	trajectory	dominant	resistant
fertile	tend	immeasurable	universe	hardy	resourceful
flourish	thrive	infinite	vast	hierarchy	stability
lush		minuscule		nomadic	

Take Students From Word Masters to Movie Scripts

I recently added this activity to my teaching repertoire and fell in love! It was created by Nancy Fetzer (2013) for her writing curriculum and is described in her free training videos (nancyfetzer.com). After teaching students three target vocabulary words from a read-aloud text, work with students to create an entirely new story that contains the same three words. You draw pictures to represent the story's beginning, middle, and end. Once you've come up with the story, support students as they orally rehearse it throughout the week. If your students are ready, have them write the story at the end of the week; and if they're not ready, keep it as an oral language activity. I highly recommend you check it out and try it out!

Strategies for Developing and Activating Background Knowledge

Prioritize Knowledge Acquisition

Don't neglect content-area instruction. Always make time to teach content areas such as science and social studies, as well as building knowledge during your literacy block. Think of comprehension instruction as a way to do that. For example, directly teach critical information before having students read a passage. Consider the strands of Scarborough's Reading Rope as you navigate texts with students. Think about how to align your work in reading and writing with your work in science, social studies, and other content areas. As I said earlier, content-area instruction should begin in kindergarten. Those five-year-olds will continue to build on their knowledge in the following school years and throughout their lives. Prioritizing knowledge acquisition will develop the knowledge our students need for college and careers, and help them to become valuable citizens of society.

Activate or Build Relevant Background Knowledge

Simply activating background knowledge at the beginning of a reading comprehension lesson is not enough. We must activate background knowledge that is specific to the text. For example, if the text you're sharing is on polar bears, you might ask students where polar bears live and what it's like there, and not about their favorite animal. Additionally, you may need to build background knowledge if students have little to no content knowledge of the topic. Stevens and Austin (2022) share a quick, practical way to build students' background knowledge before reading a text. They recommend organizing expository text passages that relate to a central unit or theme.

"Teachers can read aloud to build students' knowledge of the world beyond their scope and to help students make connections from the known to the new. There is likely no better way to draw children into the treasures stored in the written word than through reading aloud to them as much as possible."

—David Liben

1. Summarize the unit's big idea.

2. Position the new learning with students' prior learning. Help them understand how what they learned in a previous lesson connects with what they will learn in the current lesson.

3. Use a visual to support important information students need to understand the text.

4. Ask at least one comprehension question to give a purpose for reading the text.

Following those steps, here is an example of what I might say to build my students' background knowledge before reading a nonfiction book on desert animals:

> We are learning all about the different places that animals live. We read about the bayou and the animals that live there. What is the bayou like? What animals live there? Then we read about animals that live in the forest. Why is the forest a good place for those animals to live? Today we are going to read about animals that live in the desert. (Display a picture of the desert.) What do you notice about this picture of the desert? What do you think it's like there? What animals do you think live in the desert? Let's read our book together to find out.

Generate Questions

Teaching students to generate and answer their own questions about the text encourages them to process that text more actively (NRP, 2000). Questions can range from literal to inferential. I generally start with the literal questions, writing *who*, *what*, *where*, *when*, *why*, and *how* on the board. Then, after reading a page or two of our text together, I might ask, "Who can think of a

who question about this page? Who can think of a *when* question?" and so on. Generating questions takes practice. If students struggle with it, take things to the sentence level by showing them how to flip a statement into a question. For example, I read the following sentence to my students: "Frogs live at the pond." Then I model how to flip that statement into a question: "Where do frogs live?" After I model, I give students another statement and have them practice flipping it into a question with a partner. I can scaffold this further by telling them which question word to use (i.e., *who*, *what*, *where*, *when*, *why*, or *how*). Once they get the hang of generating a statement into a question, I have them generate questions from a page or the entire text.

Summarize

When we've finished a text, my students and I generate and answer questions about the whole text. I write the question words on the board and from there, for fiction, ask, "*Who* were the main characters of the story? *Where* did the story take place? *When* did the story happen? *What* was the main problem the characters faced? *How* was the problem solved? We answer the questions together and I write the answers under the relevant question word. Then, I model summarizing the text using our answers to the questions. Students then orally summarize the text with their partners. I might also have them write their summaries. From there, I might have them shrink their summaries to just 10 words. It's a great way for students to narrow in on the most critical concepts of the text.

who: Frog and Toad
where: meadow, woods
when: afternoon
what: Toad lost his button.
how: Frog helps him find it.

Watch a whole-class summarizing exercise.

Paragraph Shrinking

Paragraph shrinking, developed as one of the Peer Assisted Learning Strategies (PALS; Fuchs et al., 2001) by Vanderbilt University, is an excellent way for students to attend to meaning while they read and summarize the main points of a paragraph. This strategy can be used with the whole class, in small groups, or in pairs. I especially love to use it as part of a partner reading routine, described on page 123. It requires lots of teacher modeling and scaffolded practice. It is an evidence-based activity that helps students determine the main idea of a text. Here are the steps:

Sample paragraph:

> But there's an important reason behind the sloth's slow pace. Sloths normally just eat leaves and twigs. This doesn't give them a whole lot of energy to spend. So one way their bodies have adapted is by moving slowly. This helps them save energy. ("A Slow-Moving Sloth," 2018)

After reading a paragraph, ask the student to:

1. Name the most important who or what. In this case, the *who* is the sloth.

2. Say the most important thing about the who or what. For example, the most important thing about the sloth is that it doesn't get much energy from the food it eats, so it moves really slowly to save energy.

3. Say the main idea in 10 words or less. For instance, "The reason sloths move slowly is to save their energy."

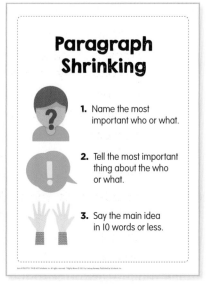

Adapted from PALS Program by Fuchs et al. (2001)

Offer Retrieval Practice

Retrieval practice means recalling information to your mind, without having it in front of you. Cognitive researchers have found that a significant amount of learning occurs when students pull information "out" through retrieval practice (Agarwal, n.d.). Small tweaks to your teaching can have a big impact on students' learning. Here are three quick tips for implementing retrieval practice. (Agarwal, n.d.).

Retrieve: Rather than starting class by recapping content ("Here's what we did in class last week"), simply ask students to retrieve ("What did we do in class last week?").

Brain Dumps: Ask students to write down quickly everything they can remember from a previous lesson.

Two Things: Ask students to retrieve two things they learned at the end of class.

To learn more about retrieval practice, check out *Powerful Teaching* by Pooja K. Agarwal and Patrice M. Bain.

In Closing, Remember...

- Reading comprehension is complex and multifaceted.
- The most important factor in good reading comprehension is how much vocabulary and content knowledge you have of the subject.
- There is no comprehension strategy powerful enough to compensate for the fact that you can't read the words (Archer, 2011).
- Support comprehension by making time for social studies and science instruction.
- Integrate content-building in your literacy block.
- Rich read-alouds help students see alternative perspectives, think critically, and learn new information.
- Using multiple texts on the same topic is a great way to deepen knowledge and vocabulary acquisition.
- Wide-reading allows students to gain information about our world, build content knowledge, learn words, consider new perspectives, and gain new insights
- Support comprehension by having students generate questions and practice paragraph shrinking.
- Intentionally teaching vocabulary words with a systematic routine before students encounter them in a text will allow them to comprehend both the text and the words better.
- Support vocabulary development by using sophisticated language, having students create 3-column notes, allowing them to act out words in skits, and having them write stories using their targeted words.
- Students can deepen their knowledge by writing about what they read.

KEEP Viewing comprehension as the overall goal and outcome of reading.

STOP Expecting that spending extensive time on isolated comprehension skills will improve reading comprehension.

START Building background knowledge and prioritizing explicit vocabulary instruction.

Conclusion

Seven years ago, when my son was in kindergarten, he drew me this picture. It depicts the two of us flying drones together on a train track, with this message: "I love you, Mom."

The signs of dyslexia were there, but I didn't see them. I didn't even know them back then. He spelled the word *love* using the letters he knew were in the word *of*. He remembered that *of* has an *o* and *f*, but he couldn't remember the order because he hadn't mapped those letters and sounds. And he often mixed up letter names, so to write *you* he used a *y* instead of the letter *u*. I can see the struggle and effort my son put into this message, and it brings up such tender emotions.

This picture reminds me not only of the struggles he has experienced, but also of how far he has come. I started working with him as he was finishing third grade. We rarely missed a day that summer, and I continued working with him through the school years. By fifth grade, he had caught up with his peers in his accuracy. And at the end of sixth grade, based on a quick assessment I gave him, he read *140 words correct per minute* with 100 percent accuracy on a sixth-grade passage. Benchmark is 120. I cried. I was so proud of him. While I wish I had understood how to help him in kindergarten, I am thankful that I eventually learned what to do. His picture reminds me of the triumphs, the silver linings, and the unbreakable connection the two of us have. I think of cuddling on the couch as he reads aloud to me. I think of him coming into my classroom, relief on his face, ready to work with me... a respite from the storm. I think of the times he has told me how much he loves reading. I think of catching him late at night, reading under the covers... and how upset he became when I said, "Lights out!"

His picture reminds me of the teacher I was and the teacher I am now. I think of everything I've learned and applied in my classroom. I think of all the students I've been able to help... because of my son. I have not only improved my reading instruction for my struggling students, but for all my students.

His picture also reminds me of the other people out there, just like him—those struggling in that sea of words. Who will help them navigate the storm? We will. Now that we know how, we can assist others in this difficult journey.

I hope that by sharing my thinking, I have inspired you to reconsider your own thinking. And because science is always evolving, rethinking what we do in our classrooms is an ongoing process. It enables us to refine and improve our techniques constantly as we implement research in the best ways we can.

Teaching is one of the greatest careers in the world. We make such a difference in the lives of our students every single day. Using the science of reading to provide them with effective instruction is the greatest gift we can give them. The ability to read opens up countless opportunities for them. We can make that happen. I hope this book inspires you to implement the 7 Mighty Moves in your classroom.

References

Adams, M. J. (1998). The three-cueing system. In F. Lehr & J. Osborn (Eds.), *Literacy for all issues in teaching and learning* (pp. 73–99). The Guilford Press.

Adams, M. J. (2020). *Theory & Practice*. Straight Talk Live Virtual Conference, Online May 20, 2020. Step by Step Learning.

Agarwal, P. (n.d.). *What is retrieval practice?* Unleash Learning. Retrieved November 27, 2022, from https://www.retrievalpractice.org/

Archer, A. L. (2022). Explicit instruction. Safe and Civil Schools National Conference.

Archer, A. L., & Hughes, C. A. (2011). *Explicit instruction: Effective and efficient teaching (What works for special-needs learners.)* The Guilford Press.

Archer, A. L. [Center for Dyslexia MTSU]. (2019, April 19). *Why explicit instruction?* [Video]. YouTube. https://www.youtube.com/watch?v=i-qNpFtcynl

Ardoin, S. P., Morena, L. S., Binder, K. S., & Foster, T. E. (2013). Examining the impact of feedback and repeated readings on oral reading fluency: Let's not forget prosody. *School Psychology Quarterly, 28*(4), 391–404.

Armbruster, B. B., Lehr, F., & Osborn, J. (2001). *Put reading first: Kindergarten through grade 3* (The research building blocks for teaching children to read). National Institute for Literacy.

Ball, E. W., & Blachman, B. A. (1991). Does phoneme awareness training in kindergarten make a difference in early word recognition and developmental spelling? *Reading Research Quarterly, 26*(1), 49–66.

Beck, I. L., & McKeown, M. G. (2001). Text talk: Capturing the benefits of read-aloud experiences for young children. *The Reading Teacher, 55*(1), 10–20.

Beck, I. L., McKeown, M. G., & Kucan, L. (2013). *Bringing words to life, second edition: Robust vocabulary.* The Guilford Press.

Berkeley, S., Scruggs, T. E., & Mastropieri, M. A. (2009). Reading comprehension instruction for students with learning disabilities, 1995–2006: A meta-analysis. *Remedial and Special Education, 31*(6), 423–436.

Berninger, V. W., & Wolf, B. J. (2015). *Teaching students with dyslexia, dysgraphia, OWL LD, and dyscalculia* (2nd ed.). Brookes Publishing.

Birsh, J. R. (2018). *Multisensory teaching of basic language skills* (1st ed.). Brookes Publishing.

Blachman, B. A. (1995). *Identifying the core linguistic deficits and the critical conditions for early intervention with children with reading disabilities*. Paper presented at the annual meeting of the Learning Disabilities Association, Orlando, FL, March 1995.

Blachman, B. A., Tangel, D. M., Ball, E. W., Black, R., & McGraw, C. K. (1999). Developing phonological awareness and word recognition skills: A two-year intervention with low-income, inner-city children. *Reading and Writing: An Interdisciplinary Journal, 11*, 239–273.

Blevins, W. (2023). *Phonics from A to Z: A practical guide* (4th ed). Scholastic.

Boyer, N., & Ehri, L. C. (2011). Contribution of phonemic segmentation instruction with letters and articulation pictures to word reading and spelling in beginners. *Scientific Studies of Reading, 15*(5), 440–470.

Brady, S. (2020). A 2020 perspective on research findings on alphabetics (phoneme awareness and phonics): Implications for instruction. *The Reading League, 3*(September/October), 20–28.

Burns, M. K., Karich, A. C., Maki, K. E., Anderson, A., Pulles, S. M., Ittner, A., McComas, J. J., & Helman, L. (2015). Identifying classwide problems in reading with screening data. *Journal of Evidence Based Practice in Schools, 14* (2), 186–204.

Cain, K. (2009). Making sense of text: Skills that support text comprehension and its development. *Perspectives on Language and Literacy, 35*(2), 11–14.

Carreker, S. (2003). Oral language and listening comprehension [Kit]. Neuhaus Education Center Press.

Castiglioni-Spalten, M. L., & Ehri, L. C. (2003). Phonemic awareness instruction: Contribution of articulatory segmentation to novice beginners' reading and spelling. *Scientific Studies of Reading, 7*(1), 25–52.

Castles, A., Rastle, K., & Nation, K. (2018). Ending the reading wars: Reading acquisition from novice to expert. *Psychological Science in the Public Interest, 19*(1), 5–51.

Catts, H. W., Nielsen, D. C., Bridges, M. S., & Liu, Y. S. (2016). Early identification of reading comprehension difficulties. *Journal of Learning Disabilities, 49*(5), 451–465.

Cervetti, G. N., & Hiebert, E. H. (2018). Knowledge at the center of English language arts instruction. *The Reading Teacher, 72*(4), 499–507.

Chafouleas, S. M., Martens, B. K., Dobson, R. L., Weinstein, K. S., & Gardner, K. B. (2004). Fluent reading as the improvement of stimulus control: Additive effects of performance-based interventions to repeated reading on students' reading and error rates. *Journal of Behavioral Education, 13*(2), 67–81.

Connor, C. M., Morrison, F. J., & Underwood, P. S. (2007). A second chance in second grade: The independent and cumulative impact of first- and second-grade reading instruction and students' letter-word reading skill growth. *Scientific Studies of Reading, 11*(3), 199–233.

Cooper, J. D., Boschken, I., McWilliams, J., & Pistochini, L. (2000). A study of the effectiveness of an intervention program designed to accelerate reading for struggling readers in the upper grades. In T. Shanahan & F. V. Rodriguez-Brown (Eds.), *49th yearbook of the National Reading Conference* (pp. 477–486). National Reading Conference.

Dehaene, S. (2010). *Reading in the brain: The new science of how we read (Reprint ed.).* Penguin Books.

Department for Education. (2017, December 5). *Pupils in England climb global rankings in reading and literacy.* GOV.UK. https://www.gov.uk/government/news/pupils-in-england-climb-global-rankings-in-reading-and-literacy

Duke, N. K., & Cartwright, K. B. (2021). The science of reading progresses: Communicating advances beyond the simple view of reading. *Reading Research Quarterly, 56*(S1), S25–S44.

Ecalle, J., Dujardin, E., Gomes, C., Cros, L., & Magnan, A. (2021). Decoding, fluency and reading comprehension: Examining the nature of their relationships in a large-scale study with first graders. *Reading & Writing Quarterly, 37*(5), 444–461.

Ehri, L. C. (2003). Systematic phonics instruction: Findings of the National Reading Panel.

Ehri, L. C. (2004). Teaching phonemic awareness and phonics: An explanation of the national reading panel meta-analyses. In P. McCardle & V. Chhabra (Eds.), *The voice of evidence in reading research* (pp. 153–186). Brookes Publishing.

Ehri, L. C. (2014). Orthographic mapping in the acquisition of sight word reading, spelling memory, and vocabulary learning. *Scientific Studies of Reading 18*(1), 5–21. P6.

Ehri, L. C. (2020). The science of learning to read words: A case for systematic phonics instruction. *Reading Research Quarterly, 55*(S1).

Ehri, L. C., Nunes, S. R., Stahl, S. A., & Willows, D. M. (2001). Systematic phonics instruction helps students learn to read: Evidence from the National Reading Panel's meta-analysis. *Review of Educational Research, 71*(3), 393–447.

Eldredge, J. L. (1993). *Decoding strategies* (1st ed.). Kendall Hunt Publishing.

Elleman, A. M., Lindo, E. J., Morphy, P., & Compton, D. L. (2009). The impact of vocabulary instruction on passage-level comprehension of school-age children: A meta-analysis. *Journal of Research on Educational Effectiveness, 2*(1), 1–44.

Ellery, V., Oczkus, L., & Rasinski, T. V. (2015). *Literacy strong all year long: Powerful lessons for K–2.* International Literacy Association.

Farrell, L., & Hunter, M. (2021, October 16). *Decodable Text Linda Farrell Michael Hunter Oct 2021* [Video]. YouTube. https://www.youtube.com/watch?v=1ANZdw7-0J0

Farris, M. (2018, June 18). *Dyslexia found in high numbers in prisoners.* 4WWL. https://www.wwltv.com/article/news/local/dyslexia-found-in-high-numbers-in-prison/289-565432758

Fetzer, N. (2013). *Nancy Fetzer's writing curriculum grades K–1.* Nancy Fetzer's Literacy Connections.

Flood, J., Lapp D., & Fisher, D. (2005). Neurological impress Method PLUS, *Reading Psychology, 26*(2), 147–160.

Fowler, A. E. (1991). How early phonological development might set the state for phoneme awareness. In S. A. Brady & D. P. Shankweiler (Eds.), *Phonological processes in literacy* (pp.97–117). Erlbaum.

Fuchs, D., Fuchs, L. S., Otaiba, S. A., Thompson, A., Yen, L., Mcmaster, K. N., Svenson, E., & Yang, N. J. (2001). K-PALS helping kindergartners with reading readiness: Teachers and researchers in partnerships. *Teaching Exceptional Children, 33*(4), 76–80.

Fuchs, D., Fuchs, L. S., Simmons, D., & Mathes, P. (2008). *Peer assisted learning strategies: Reading methods for grades 2–6.* Vanderbilt University.

Gillingham, A., & Stillman, B. W. (1997). *The Gillingham manual: Remedial training for students with specific disability in reading, spelling, and penmanship* (8th ed.). Educators Pub Svc Inc.

Goldberg, M. (2021, June). *What do I do with all these predictable books?* Right to Read Project. https://righttoreadproject.com/2021/06/19/what-do-i-do-with-all-these-predictable-books/

Gonzalez-Frey, S. M., & Ehri, L. C. (2020). Connected phonation is more effective than segmented phonation for teaching beginning readers to decode unfamiliar words. *Scientific Studies of Reading, 25*(3), 272–285.

Goodman, K. S. (1967). Reading: A psycholinguistic guessing game. *Journal of the Reading Specialist, 6*(4), 126–135.

Grace, K. (2005). *Phonics and spelling through phoneme-grapheme mapping.* Sopris West.

Graham, S., Harris, K. R., & Santangelo, T. (2015). Research-based writing practices and the Common Core: Meta-analysis and meta-synthesis. *The Elementary School Journal, 115*(4), 498–522.

Graham, S., & Hebert, M. A. (2010). *Writing to read: Evidence for how writing can improve reading.* A Report from Carnegie Corporation of New York. Alliance for Excellent Education.

Graham, S., & Perin, D. (2007). *Writing next: Effective strategies to improve writing of adolescents in middle and high schools.* A Report to Carnegie Corporation of New York. Alliance for Excellent Education.

Hanford, E. (2019, August 22). *At a loss for words: How a flawed idea is teaching millions of kids to be poor readers.* APM Reports. https://www.apmreports.org/episode/2019/08/22/whats-wrong-how-schools-teach-reading

Hanna, P. R., Hanna, J. S., Hodges, R. E., & Rudorf, E. H. (1966). *Phoneme-grapheme correspondences as cues to spelling improvement.* U.S. Department of Health, Education, and Welfare/National Institute of Education.

Hasbrouck, J. (2006). For students who are not yet fluent, silent reading is not the best use of classroom time. *American Educator, 30*(2).

Hasbrouck, J. (2020). An update to the national reading panel report: What we know about fluency in 2020. *The Reading League Journal, 1*(3).

Hasbrouck, J. P., & Glaser, D. (2019). *Reading fluency: Understand, assess, teach.* Benchmark Education.

Hasbrouck, J., & Tindal, G. (2017). An update to compiled ORF norms (Technical Report No. 1702). Eugene, OR. Behavioral Research and Teaching, University of Oregon.

Heckelman, R. G. (1969). A neurological-impress method of remedial-reading instruction. *Academic Therapy, 4*(4), 277–282.

Hempenstall, K. (2002). The three cueing system: Help or hindrance. *Direct Instruction News, 2*(2), 42–51.

Hempenstall, K. (2006). The three-cueing model: Down for the count? *Education News.* https://www.readingrockets.org/sites/default/files/The-Three-Cueing-Model-Down-for-the-Count.pdf

Hennessy, N., & Moats, L. C. (2020). *The reading comprehension blueprint: Helping students make meaning from text.* Brookes Publishing.

Hirsch, E. D. (2003). Reading comprehension requires knowledge—of words and the world. *American Educator, 27*(1), 10, 12–13, 16–22, 28–29, 44.

Hochman, J. C., & Wexler, N. (2017). *The writing revolution: A guide to advancing thinking through writing in all subjects and grades* (1st ed.). Jossey-Bass.

Hudson, R. F., Anderson, E. M., McGraw, M., Ray, R., & Wilhelm, A. (2022). Structured literacy interventions for reading fluency. In L. Spear-Swerling (Ed.), *Structure literacy interventions* (pp. 102–107). The Guilford Press.

Hudson, R. F., Lane, H. B., & Pullen, P. C. (2005, May). Reading fluency assessment and instruction: What, why, and how? *The Reading Teacher, 58*(8), 702–714.

Hulme, C., Bowyer-Crane, C., Carroll, J. M., Duff, F. J., & Snowling, M. J. (2012). The causal role of phoneme awareness and letter-sound knowledge in learning to read. *Psychological Science, 23*(6), 572–577.

International Dyslexia Association. (2014). *IDA dyslexia handbook: What every family should know* [Electronic handbook]. Retrieved from https://dyslexiaida.org/ida-dyslexia-handbook/

Jones, C. D., Clark, S. K., & Reutzel, D. R. (2012). Enhancing alphabet knowledge instruction: Research implications and practical strategies for early childhood educators. *Early Childhood Education Journal, 41*(2), 81–89.

Juel, C., & Roper/Schneider, D. (1985). The influence of basal readers on first grade reading. *Reading Research Quarterly, 20*(2), 134.

Kame'enui, E. J., & Baumann, J. F. (2012). *Vocabulary: Research to practice* (2nd ed.). The Guilford Press.

Kilpatrick, D. A. (2015). *Essentials of assessing, preventing, and overcoming reading difficulties (Essentials of Psychological Assessment)* (1st ed.). John Wiley & Sons.

Kilpatrick, D. A. (2016). *Equipped for reading success: A comprehensive, step-by-step program for developing phonemic awareness and fluent word recognition.* Casey & Kirsch Publishers.

Kilpatrick, D. A., & O'Brien, S. (2019). Effective prevention and intervention for word-level reading difficulties. In: D. Kilpatrick, R. Joshi, & R. Wagner (Eds.), *Reading development and difficulties.* Springer.

The Kindergarten Readers. (2017, April 24). *Blending and phoneme segmentation songs* [Video]. YouTube. https://www.youtube.com/watch?v=ma29BoCHlXM

Lane, H. B., & Allen, S. A. (2010). The vocabulary-rich classroom: Modeling sophisticated word use to promote word consciousness and vocabulary growth. *The Reading Teacher, 63*(5), 362–370.

Lane, H. B., & Pullen, P. C. (2004). *Phonological awareness assessment and instruction: A sound beginning.* Allyn & Bacon.

Lee, J., & Yoon, S. Y. (2017). The effects of repeated reading on reading fluency for students with reading disabilities. *Journal of Learning Disabilities, 50*(2), 213–224.

Liben, D. (n.d.). 'Both and' literacy instruction K–5: A proposed paradigm shift for the Common Core State Standards ELA classroom. Retrieved from https://achievethecore.org/file/1204

McGuinness, D. (1999). *Why our children can't read and what we can do about it: A scientific revolution in reading* (1st ed.). Free Press.

McKeown, M. G. (2019). Effective vocabulary instruction fosters knowing words: Using words, and understanding how words work. *Language, Speech, and Hearing Services in Schools, 50*(4), 466–476.

McKeown, M. G., Beck, I. L., Omanson, R. C., & Pople, M. T. (1985). Some effects of the nature and frequency of vocabulary instruction on the knowledge and use of words. *Reading Research Quarterly, 20*(5), 522.

Mesmer, H. (2001) Decodable text: A review of what we know. *Reading Research and Instruction, 40*(2) 121–141.

Miles, K. P., & Ehri, L. C. (2017). Learning to read words on flashcards: Effects of sentence contexts and word class in native and nonnative English-speaking kindergartners. *Early Childhood Research Quarterly, 41*, 103–113.

Miles, K. P., & Ehri, L. C. (2019). *Orthographic mapping facilitates sight word memory and vocabulary learning.* Springer.

Miles, K. P., & Ehri, L. C. (2019) *Reading development and difficulties: Bridging the gap between research and practice* (pp. 63–82). Springer.

Miles, K. P., Rubin, G. B., & Gonzalez-Frey, S. (2017). Rethinking sight words. *The Reading Teacher, 71*(6), 715–726.

Moats, L. C. (1998). Teaching decoding. *American Educator, 22* (1 & 2), 42–49, 95–96.

Moats, L. C., & Foorman, B. R. (2003). Measuring teachers' content knowledge of language and reading. *Annals of Dyslexia, 53*(1), 23–45.

Moats, L. C. (2005). How spelling supports reading. *American Educator, Winter 2005/06,* 12–43.

Moats, L. C., & Tolman, C. (2019). *Language essentials for teachers of reading and spelling (LETRS) Units* 1–4 (3rd ed., Vol. 1). Voyager Sopris Learning.

Moats, L. C. (2019, October 16). *Of 'hard words' and straw men: Let's understand what reading science is really about.* Voyager Sopris Learning.

Moats, L. C. (2020). *Speech to print: Language essentials for teachers* (3rd ed.). Brookes Publishing.

Moats, L. C. (2022, June). *What do phonemes have to do with it?* [Webinar]. PaTTAN Literacy Symposium, Harrisburg, PA. https://www.youtube.com/watch?v=Jr1BRTcM8HI https://www.voyagersopris.com/blog/edview360/2019/10/16/lets-understand-what-reading-science-is-really-about

National Reading Panel (2000). *Teaching children to read: An evidence-based assessment of the scientific research on reading and its implications for reading instruction.* National Institute of Child Health and Human Development.

Orkin, M., Vanacore, K., Rhinehart, L., Gotlieb, R., & Wolf, M. (2022). The more you know: How teaching multiple aspects of word knowledge builds fluency skills. *The Reading League Journal, 3*(2).

Palinscar, A. S., & Brown, A. L. (1984). Reciprocal teaching of comprehension-fostering and comprehension-monitoring activities. *Cognition and Instruction, 1*(2), 117–175.

Parker, D. C., & Burns, M. K. (2014). Using the instructional level as a criterion to target reading interventions. *Reading & Writing Quarterly, 30*(1), 79–94.

Pearson, P. D., & Gallagher, M. C. (1983). The instruction of reading comprehension. *Contemporary Educational Psychology, 8*(3), 317–344.

Peck, M. A. "The importance of oral language in literacy and the impact on third-grade student writing" (2022). *Theses and Dissertations.* 355. https://scholar.stjohns.edu/cgi/viewcontent.cgi?article=1361&context=theses_dissertations

Perfetti, C. A. (1995). Cognitive research can inform reading education. *Journal of Research in Reading, 18*(2), 106–115.

Piasta, S. B. (2022). *Building a science of early literacy instruction: The science of alphabet instruction*. Society for the Scientific Study of Reading Annual Conference. https://www.triplesr.org/twenty-ninth-annual-sssr-conference

Piasta, S. B., & Wagner, R. K. (2010). Developing early literacy skills: A meta-analysis of alphabet learning and instruction. *Reading Research Quarterly, 45*, 8–38.

Primary National Strategy (2006). *Phonics and early reading: An overview for headteachers, literacy leaders and teachers in schools, and managers and practitioners in Early Years settings.* UK: Department of Education and Skills.

Puliatte, A., & Ehri, L. C. (2017). Do 2nd and 3rd grade teachers' linguistic knowledge and instructional practices predict spelling gains in weaker spellers? *Reading and Writing, 31*(2), 239–266.

Reading Horizons. (2019). *Reading horizons discovery teacher's manual, Chapter 1* (7th ed.).

Recht, D. R., & Leslie, L. (1988). Effect of prior knowledge on good and poor readers' memory of text. *Journal of Educational Psychology, 80*(1), 16–20.

Roberts, B. R. T., MacLeod, C. M., & Fernandes, M. A. (2022). The enactment effect: A systematic review and meta-analysis of behavioral, neuroimaging, and patient studies. *Psychological Bulletin, 148*(5–6), 397–434.

Sargiani, R. D. A., Ehri, L. C., & Maluf, M. R. (2021). Teaching beginners to decode consonant–vowel syllables using grapheme–phoneme subunits facilitates reading and spelling as compared with teaching whole-syllable decoding. *Reading Research Quarterly, 57*(2), 629–648.

Scanlon, D. M., Vellutino, F. R., Small, S. G., Fanuele, D. P., & Sweeney, J. M. (2005). Severe reading difficulties—Can they be prevented? A comparison of prevention and intervention approaches. *Exceptionality, 13*(4), 209–227.

Scarborough, H. (2001). Connecting early language and literacy to later reading disabilities: Evidence, theory and practice. In S. B. Neuman & D. K. Dickinson (Eds.), *Handbook of early literacy research* (Vol. 1, pp. 97–110). The Guilford Press.

Sedita, J. (2022). *The writing rope: A framework for explicit writing instruction in all subjects*. Brookes Publishing.

Seidenberg, M. (2018). *Language at the speed of sight* (Reprint ed.). Basic Books.

Seidenberg, M. (2021, November 20). Clarity about Fountas and Pinnell. *Reading Matters*. https://seidenbergreading.net/2021/11/20/clarity-about-fountas-and-pinnell/

Shanahan, T., & Lonigan, C. J. (2010). The National Early Literacy Panel. *Educational Researcher, 39*(4), 279–285.

Shanahan, T. (2017, June 18). *Is building knowledge the best way to increase literacy achievement?* Shanahan on Literacy. 9. www.shanahanonliteracy.com/blog/is-building-knowledge-the-best-way-to-increase-literacy-achievement#sthash.KC1qMvZg.dpbs

Shapiro, A. (2004). How including prior knowledge as a subject variable may change outcomes of learning research. *American Educational Research Journal, 41*(1), 159–189.

Smith, R., Snow, P., Serry, T., & Hammond, L. (2021). The role of background knowledge in reading comprehension: A critical review. *Reading Psychology, 42*(3), 214–240.

Snider, V. E. (1995). A primer on phonemic awareness: What it is, why it's important, and how to teach it. *School Psychology Review, 24*(3), 443–455.

Snow, C. E., & Juel, C. (2005). Teaching children to read: What do we know about how to do it? In M. J. Snowling & C. Hulme (Eds.), *The science of reading: A handbook* (pp. 501–520). Blackwell Publishing.

Stahl, S. A., & Fairbanks, M. M. (1986). The effects of vocabulary instruction: A model-based meta-analysis. *Review of Educational Research, 56*(1), 72–110.

Stanovich, K. E. (1988). Explaining the differences between the dyslexic and the garden-variety poor reader. *Journal of Learning Disabilities, 21*(10), 590–604.

Stevens, E., & Austin, C. (2022). Structured reading comprehension intervention for students with reading difficulties. In L. Spear-Swerling (Ed.), *Structured literacy interventions* (pp. 165–167). The Guilford Press.

Stollar, S. (2020, June). Every word wants to be a sight word when it grows up. *Reading Science Academy*. https://www.readingscienceacademy.com/blog/every-word-wants-to-be-a-sight-word-when-it-grows-up

Stone, L. (2019). *Reading for life: High quality literacy instruction for all* (1st ed.). Routledge.

Torgesen, J. K. (2000). Individual differences in response to early interventions in reading: The lingering problem of treatment resisters. *Learning Disabilities Research & Practice, 15*(1), 55–64.

Torgesen, J. K. (2020, September 10). *Avoiding the devastating downward spiral*. American Federation of Teachers.

Treiman, R., & Zukowski, A. (1991). Levels of phonological awareness. In S. A. Brady & D. P. Shankweiler (Eds.), *Phonological processes in literacy* (pp. 67–83). Erlbaum.

Treiman, R. (2017). Learning to spell words: Findings, theories, and issues. *Scientific Studies of Reading, 21*(4), 265–276.

Tunmer, W. E., Chapman, J. W., & Prochnow, J. E. (2004). Why the reading achievement gap in New Zealand won't go away: Evidence from the PIRLS 2001 International Study of Reading Achievement. *New Zealand Journal of Educational Studies, 39*(1), 127–145.

Vellutino, F. R., Fletcher, J. M., Snowling, M. J., & Scanlon, D. M. (2004). Specific reading disability (dyslexia): what have we learned in the past four decades? *Journal of Child Psychology and Psychiatry, 45*(1), 2–40.

Weaver, C. (1988). *Reading process & practice: From socio-psycholinguistics to whole language*. Heinemann.

Weeden, T. (2022). *Literacy as a human right*. PaTTAN Literacy Symposium 2022, United States of America. https://www.pattan.net/Videos/Keynote-Literacy-as-a-Human-Right-2022-Literacy-Sy

Wexler, N. (2020). Th*e knowledge gap: The hidden cause of America's broken education system—and how to fix it*. Avery.

Wolf, M. (2008). *Proust and the squid: The story and science of the reading brain* (Reprint). Harper Perennial.

Yoncheva, Y. N., Wise, J., & McCandliss, B. (2015). Hemispheric specialization for visual words is shaped by attention to sublexical units during initial learning. *Brain and Language, 145–146*, 23–33.

Index